INDUSTRIAL ENGINEERING & ORGANISATION METHODS

WITH REFERENCE TO INDUSTRIAL RELATIONS AND PERSONNEL MANAGEMENT

DR SANTHAPALLI GAUTAMI

My Father

Sri M. Ananda Prakash

Contents

Foreword

Today, companies are competing in a very different environment than they were only a few years ago. Rapid changes such as global competition, e-business, the Internet, and advances in technology have required businesses to adapt their standard practices. Operations management (OM) is the critical function through which companies can succeed in this competitive landscape.

Operations management concepts are not confined to one department. Rather, they are far-reaching, affecting every functional aspect of the organization. Whether studying accounting, finance, human resources, information technology, management, marketing, or purchasing, students need to understand the critical impact operations management has on any business.

I have more than 20 years of teaching experience and understand the challenges inherent in teaching and taking the introductory OM course. The vast majority of students taking this course are not majoring in operations management. Rather, classes are typically composed of students from various business disciplines or students who are undecided about their major and have little knowledge of operations management. The challenge is not only to teach the foundation of the field, but also to help students understand the impact operations management has on the business as a whole and the close relationship of operations management with other business functions.

I have motivated to write this book to help students understand operations management and production management otherwise called Industrial Engineering & Organisation Methods with reference to Industrial Relations and Personnel Management.

Dr. Santhapalli Gautami

Date: 1st October 2022

Preface

It is traditional that a book of instruction be filled with rules on how to and how not to, and this book does not follow that tradition. There are no golden rules for the production manager, each production establishes its own set of rules, which continue to evolve for the duration of the tour.

Because every production is original, it has to be treated like a prototype to a certain extent, and the guidelines have to be altered to meet the requirements of each particular production. What works for one tour may not be valid for another, although there may well be several common elements. This book concentrates on the common elements.

This book specifically deals with the business of production and sets out guidelines that have to be followed by students, research scholars, academitiance and industrialist for the deep insite of purpose of this book titled Industrial Engineering & Organisation Methods with reference to Industrial Relations and Personnel Management consist of Industrial Engineering – Principles and Concepts , Productivity, Work Study – Method Study, Time Study, Application of Work Study Technique, Motion Economy, Ergonomics Mechanisation and Automation, Quality Control – 1, Quality Control – 2, The Role of OR, Modelling in OR, OR in Decision Making, Linear Programming, Transportation and Assignment Problems, Project planning with PERT and CPM, Queuing Theory and Simulation, Value Analysis and ABC Analysis, Office Management, Wage and Salary Administrative Strategies and Principles and General Administrative Management.

Author name: Dr. Santhapalli Gautami

Date: 1st October 2022.

Acknowledgements

It gives me an immense pleasure to express my feelings for the persons and institutions that have helped and inspired me to accomplish this research work.

I articulate my sincere thanks to Management of Sri Venkateswara Colleges, Tirupati for giving me wonderful opportunity to serve your reputed Institution.

I should render my deep sense of gratitude to Principal Dr.N.Sudhakar Reddy Garu, Head of the department of Management Studies, Colleagues, Friends and Students of Sri Venkateswara College of Engineering for their support and encouragement during the tenure of my research work.

My sincere gratitude to my parents Sri. M. Ananda Prakash garu, Rtd. Deputy Branch Manager, A P State Financial Corporation, Tirupati and Smt. V. Nagamani garu, Rtd. Regional Inspection Officer, Board of Intermediate Education, Chittoor District, and A.P. are my perennial source of inspiration and motivation in my life. My Siblings elder sister Smt. S. Thanuja, PGT, Zoology Lecturer, AP Model School, Kurnool and my Younger Brother Sri.S. Bhanu Venkata Prasad, B.Tech, Software Engineer, Hyderabad.

I shall remain obliged to my Husband Sri. M. Vamsidhar Reddy and my son M.Yogith Sai Reddy for their moral support and constant help forever in my life.

Dr. Santhapalli Gautami

Prologue

The objectives of this "Industrial Engineering – Principles and Concepts" is to make the student understand the meaning of Industrial Engineering, its branches and the future Industrial Engineering field.

productivity chapter are to make the student understand 1) The standard of living and productivity. 2) The relation between standard of living and productivity. 3) Types of productivity and their Measurement. 4) Methods of increasing productivity i.e., what is productivity and how it can be increased.

'Work Study – Method Study' chapter is to make the student understand – (a) The meaning of work study and method study (b) The history of work study and method study (c) The relationship to productivity (d) The process of method study in detail with main concentration on the recording techniques of the facts related to the work selected for the study. (e) Objectives of work study and method study.

'Time Study' are to make the reader understand- (a) The meaning of work measurement and its objectives. (b) Techniques of work measurement, mainly Time Study (c) Finally, how a Time Study is to be conducted and the process of determining the Standard Time. i.e., in brief, the need and calculation or Standard Time.

'Application of Work-Study Techniques' is to make the student understand (a) The basic things that are to be satisfied before conducting the work study and (b) where and how Work-Study can be applied with the help of some examples and so on to explain Motion Economy, Ergonomics Mechanisation and Automation, Quality Control, the Role of OR, Modelling in OR, OR in Decision Making, Linear Programming, Transportation and Assignment Problems, Project planning with PERT and CPM, Queuing Theory and Simulation, Value Analysis and ABC Analysis, Office Management, Wage and Salary Administrative Strategies and Principles and General Administrative Management.

CHAPTER ONE

The objectives of this chapter "Industrial Engineering – Principles and Concepts" is to make the student understand the meaning of Industrial Engineering, its branches and the future Industrial Engineering field.

CONTENTS

1.1 An Introduction

1.2 Branch of Industrial Engineering

1.3 Activities of Industrial Engineering

1.4 Productivity improvement through Industrial Engineering

1.5 Place of Industrial Engineering department in the Organization

1.6 Future of Industrial Engineering

1.7 Summary

1.8 Glossary

1.9 Reference Books

1.10 Self-assessment and questions for discussion

1.11 Questions

1.1 Introduction

Starting from the days of F.W. TYLOR and F.W. Gilbert, H.L. Gantt (1882-1912), Industrial engineering has been considered as a dynamic profession. In the field of engineering, Industrial engineering is one of the fastest growing professions. In the beginning the industrial engineering work was closely associated with Motion and Time Study. It was concerned with "The fair day's pay for a fair day's work" only at the starting time. This position continued from 1903, when F.W. Taylor's Main pioneer work through 'Shop Management' paper, till 1933 when the term 'Method engineering' or 'Method study' developed by H.S. May Mard and his associates was added.

However, the area under industrial engineering is increasing day by day. This can be clarified by the following.

If we start studying the work in order to reduce the cost, we often find that many factors other than the workers influence the cost of a job. Then we immediately think of considering the sources of raw material handling. Fast production may lead to rejections. Then we start thinking of quality and quality control. As we know that unhealthy and unsafe surroundings tend to have a costly effect on production, we will start considering ventilation, heating, lighting and safety. The payment structure for a job mainly depends upon the base rate established for that job. This makes us to think of job evaluation, personnel and pay roll (salaries and wages) accounting. In estimating labour cost, we become involved with breakeven analysis, overhead costs and accounting procedures, considerations of the worker's surroundings include tools and equipment. This leads to think of purchasing. Since an ideal time of worker represents waste and idleness may be caused by scheduling, we may lead to question production control systems. And so...it runs.

Direct connection can be shown between job design, the origin of industrial engineering, and almost any function in an Industrial organization.

Because of education and training coupled with a persistent "why"? industrial engineering can enter any department of the organization. And they are the best candidates for production supervision. This creates increasing and counting demand for industrial engineers (dues to use of industrial engineer's services in every department).

So, we can define industrial engineering as "The engineering approach applied to all factors, including the human factor, involved in the production and distribution of products and services".

The analytical approach to solving management problems had led recently to new concepts of industrial engineering. Some procedures like systems engineering and operations research have been developed to deal with today's complex problems in industrial, government and military organization.

In order to reflect these concepts, we can have the following definition which is comprehensive and which also tries to define the limits of industrial engineering.

Definition given by 'American Society of Mechanical Engineering', "Industrial Engineering is concerned with the design improvement and installation of integrated system of men, materials and equipment's drawing upon specialized knowledge and skill in the mathematical, physical and social sciences together with the principles and methods of engineering analysis and design, to specify, product and evaluate the results to be obtained from such systems".

As the time passes all things get changes. The development observed until now in industrial engineering leads everyone to anticipated/expected further changes. Presently industrial engineers are working almost every area of industrial activity.

1.2 Branches of Industrial Engineering

The following are the branches of industrial engineering which explains the wide area covered under it.

1. Work study (a) Methods study

(b) Work Measurement

2. Plant layout and material handling

3. Inventory control

4. Operations Research

5. Production Planning and Control

6. Systems Engineering

7. CPM and PERT

8. Value Engineering

9. Cybernetics.

The above branches of industrial engineering will be dealt in detail in coming chapter. But before this, let us now see all of them in brief.

1. Work Study: It deals with the problems

(I) As to how should a job be done?

(ii) How much time a job should take for completion?

(iii) The answers for these two questions are-

(a) The job should be performed in the best possible way.

(b) The time taken for the job should be the least possible time (considering all the factors like times, qualified representative Works rate etc.) i. e., fixing the standard time. The above two answers are got by the techniques of work study. They are –

(1a) Method Study: The first question of work study will be answered by this. I.e., this aims at finding the best possible way of doing way of doing on job in order to maximize the usage of resources.

(1b) Work Measurement: The second question of work study will be answered by this. I. e., this aims at finding the correct time required for performing any job activity (Standard time).

(2a) Plant Layout: This is technique of locating different machines and plant services within the factory, so that each operation is performed at the point of greatest convenience and great possible output of high quality so as to have lowest possible total cost.

(2b) Material Handling: Lot of production time is consumed in handing materials before after and during the process of manufacturing. Therefore, by proper selection of operation (using) and maintenance of material handling devices, we can improve the output, the quality, speed up the deliveries and, therefore cost of production.

(3) Inventory Control: It is the systematic location, storage in such a way that desired degree of service can be made to operating shops at minimum ultimate cost.

(4) Operation Research: This is research technique, offers alternative plans for a problem, to the management for making decisions, the scientific and quantitative analysis of the problem (done by the team of statisticians, psychologists, labour specialists, mathematicians, industrial engineers etc.) is presented before the Management, to enable him to make sound decisions. This deals with the complicated problems like, queuing theory, linear programming, transportation problems, inventory control, sequential decisions, equipment replacement policy etc.

(5) Production Planning and Control: It is process of planning the production in advance, setting the exact route for each item to give production orders to shops and lastly to follow up the progress of products according to the production orders.

(6) System engineering: System engineering is the process of successfully developing large scale complex man machine systems within cost, time and performance targets. System engineer is a combination of engineer-scientist-administrator. He must take use of new and unfamiliar disciplines to achieve his objectives.

(7) CPM and PERT: These are modern net-work techniques used by the management for programming. CPM means critical path method. In this we identify most crucial/critical elements of a job. Then it helps the managers to concentrate on them so that the project can be completed.

PERT is programmed evaluation and review technique. For this we think of projects having uncertainty of exact time for each element. Then it tries to identify an estimates time in which the project can be completed.

(8) Value engineering: It is a technique used for reducing the cost of product by making changes in design, specifications of material used, source of supply tool design, machinability, tolerances etc.

(9) Cybernetics: It has been observed that there is marked similarity between the structures of classical control systems and various biological and other physical systems. Thus, cybernetics is a new engineering discipline in which biological and other physical systems are studied and then applied to engineering problems.

1.3 Activities of Industrial Engineering

The Industrial engineering field represents an area which is undergoing rapid Expansion and diversification. For example, among many activities that an industrial Engineer might be called upon to engage in, we find the following,

1. Locate new plants and design their physical layout.

2. Analyze and plan production schedules and inventories

3. Find ways to improve the productivity and moral or people at work.

4. Study the feasibility of equipment replacement.

5. Conduct effective work measurement and set the time standards for effective wage payment.

6. Utilization of digital computer to receive tremendous quantities of information to digest, process and store information, and then to display this information for appropriate decision making.

7. By applying operations research technique find out better production methods.

8. Analyze the schedule big projects by using CPM and PERT.

9. Develop and maintain standards governing administrative sales budget, including the summarizing of the sales forecasting function and the responsibility for the market analysis function.

10. Analyze, establish and control of all office, routines and procedure from a functional stand point, including their simplification, development and control and the design of management information systems.

11. Aid in establishing cost controls, performance rating charts, budgetary controls, and the like designed to fit his actual needs.

12. Assist in the development of training programmers and aid in training supervisors and workers in the proper performance or their duties.

1.4 Productivity Improvement through Industrial Engineering

All the above activities of industrial engineering, if used properly leads to increase in productivity. The productivity increase in organization leads to the ever an increase in average standard of living of the country. In order to complete in the international market, the prices are to be competitive. This is possible by an increase in productivity. Increasing productivity is also technique to check the inflation.

As productivity increases, the following benefits like salaries/earnings increase, more goods at same price, country and industry and organization will prosper etc., can be enjoyed. So, our aim should be to make people more conscious about productive increase if we want to increase the average standard of living.

Thus, we have seen that "Industrial engineering is an organized continuous effort to improve productivity and quality and to reduce costs within an organization". For this purpose, industrial engineer must continue to lend the way in "resource utilization" and he can play an important role in increasing productivity based on various factors said earlier.

1.5 Place Industrial engineering Department in the Organization:

In the organization (structure), the industrial department must be given a high position or places in one of top levels, so that the persons working in this department cannot be influenced by workers and lower-level managers and the suggestions given by these persons will be accepted with respect and they will be implemented.

Since the industrial engineering department is meant for providing service to the management of the organization, it is suggested to have this department as Staff function rather than Line function, I. e., they have no authority to give orders but they can suggest.

The position of the head of the Industrial Engineering department in relation to his fellow members of the staff depends upon following important factors.

1. Size of organization

2. Type of organization and whether managed by owner himself or by professions.

3. Nature of work carried out it the factory, qualifications, experience and personality etc., of the chief industrial engineer and those of other departmental heads.

Looking to above factors there cannot be any standard chart for organizational structure. A typical organization chart showing the position of industrial engineering Department is given here under.

Sometimes Chief Industrial Engineer is given a place under works manager. It is due to reason that Works Manager is responsible to increase the overall Productivity by putting the Industrial Engineering Department under him; he can give more importance to thane suggestions or advices placed before him. In such case the organizational structure will be similar to that shown in the chart below.

1.6 Future of Industrial Engineering

For our country, with large population and high growth rate of population we need to develop rapidly. For this purpose, we have to economies wherever it is possible by giving due, consideration to industrial engineering.

In order to have a root in our country for engineering, our immediate work to be performed is to provide educational facilities in the universities and colleges. We must also run short duration courses with the help of industries. This is needed for

(I) Existing industrial engineers to make them familiar with the latest development in the field, and

(ii) Other staff members to important basic knowledge of the activities of industrial engineering.

There is also for the massive and continuous research and development to get facts which we do not yet have productivity measurement methods must be evolved in the production field as we as in the service sector specially where it is extremely difficult to measure the work we must put more time, money and effort for positive encouragement of productivity improvement. Concentrated efforts must also be made to remove many of the roadblocks and restrictions of productivity improvement which presently exists.

In making the industrial engineering popular, it is moral duty of the existing Industrial Engineers to convince the Top management (with their work) that money spent on their salary and projects is one of the best investments which a company makes, and that industrial engineering department is an excellent investment and not just added over head. To justify their existence, they must give a high return of investment made on them.

1.7 Summary

In the initial stages industrial engineering was used as sinuous to motion and time study. This continued until the term method study was introduced. The field of Industrial Engineering is expanding day by day. To have the present picture about the Industrial Engineering we can see the following definition.

"Industrial engineering is concerned with the design, improvement and installation of integrated system of men, materials and equipment's drawing upon specialized knowledge and skill in the mathematical, physical and social sciences together with the principles and methods of engineering analysis and design, to specify, predict and evaluate the results to be obtained from such systems".

The following are the branches of the Industrial Engineering which explain the limits of it (a) Work Study (b) Plant lay out Material handling (c) Inventory control (d) Operations research (e) Production planning and control (f) Systems Engineering (g) CPM and PERT (h) Value Engineering (I) Cybernetics.

The main aim of industrial engineering is to increase the prosperity of the organization and country / Society by increasing productivity, quality and decreasing costs.

In the organization structure it is suggested to place the Industrial Engineering department as Staff position rather than line position as they are meant for helping the management. There is no one single, standard organization chart to show the position of this department but we can have some typical examples.

For our country we need to emphasize more on industrial engineering as we need rapid development.

1.8 Glossary

Industrial Engineering: The engineering approach applied to all factors, including human factors, involved in the production and distribution of products and services.

Line authority: A person is said to be having line authority of he is having right to give orders.

Staff authority: A person is said to be in staff position if he is having no authority to give orders but can give suggestions.

1.9 Reference Books

1. T. R. Banga, N. K. Agarwal, S. C. Sharma, Industrial Engineering and Management Publish eScience, Khanna Publishers, Delhi o1989. 1 to 7

2. Richard McVaugh's, Introduction to industrial engineering. The lowa state university press, USA, Second edition. Pages 5-9, 33 and 34.

3. W. Grant Ireson and Engine L. Grant, Hand book of Industrial Engineering and Management, Prentice Hall of India Private limited, New Delhi, 1917 pages 1121-1183.

1.10 Self-assessment and Questions for discussion

1) Discuss the difference between industrial Engineering and Motion and Time and Study?

2) Discuss how the industrial engineering is necessary for India in order to have rapid development?

1.11 Questions

1) What are the branches of industrial engineering. Discuss them briefly?

2) What is Industrial engineering? What are the activities of Industrial engineering?

Productivity

The objectives of this productivity chapter are to make the student understand.

1) The standard of living and productivity.

2) The relation between standard of living and productivity.

3) Types of productivity and their Measurement

4) Methods of increasing productivity i.e., what is productivity and how it can be increased.

CONTENTS

2.1 The Standard of living.

2.2 Requirements for a minimum satisfactory standard of living.

2.3 Productivity definition and meaning.

2.4 Basic Types of productivity.

2.5 Benefits of higher productivity in organization.

2.6 Measurement of labour productivity.

2.7 Capital productivity Measurement

2.8 Management productivity

2.9 Summary

2.10 Glossary

2.11 Reference books

2.12 Self-assessment

2.13 Discussion and project work

2.1 The Standard of living

The standard of living means the degree of material well-being available to person or class or community, which is necessary for sustaining and enjoying life.

The standard of living of the representative person or family widely varies from country and even within the country for community to community. In spite of many efforts made at the national and international levels, even today a large portion of people continue to be in actuate poverty condition.

2.2 Requirements for a minimum satisfactory standard of living

The followings are basic requirement for a human being in order to minimum decent standard of living:

1) Enough food every day to replace the energy used in living and working.

2) Enough CLOTHING to protect the boxy from the whether

3) SHELTER with some household equipment and furniture to have protection under healthy conditions.

4) SECURITY against robbery or violence, against loss of job or work, against poverty due to illness or old age and.

5) ESSENTIAL SERVICES such as safe drinking water, sanitation, medical care, public transport and educational and cultural facilities that would permit every human being to develop his talent and abilities to the maximum.

2.3 Productivity definition and Meaning:

Productivity is a measure of economic or business performance that indicates how efficiently people, companies, industries and whole economies convert inputs, such as labor and capital, into outputs, such as goods or services.

Productivity is the state of being able to create, particularly at a high quality and quick speed. An example of productivity is being able to make top notch school projects in a limited amount of time. An example of productivity is how quickly a toy factory is able to produce toys.

Productivity is a measure of how efficiently a person completes a task. We can define it as the rate at which a company or country produces goods and services (output), usually judged based on the amounts of inputs (labor, capital, energy, or other resources) used to deliver those goods and services.

Productivity implies the quantitative relationship between what is produced (output) and how many resources are used during production (input). In other words, it is the ratio between the output of goods and the input of resources consumed. Hence, an increase in productivity indicates an increase in output, which is proportionately higher than the increase in input.

Symbolically, it can be expressed as:

Input refers to the use of all the resources for the creation of goods and services. As against, the output is the quantity of goods and services produced. It can be expressed in terms of production in relation to time units. Therefore, it increases production and decreases cost.

Productivity is a philosophy of life, a state of mind. Being efficient means doing, at every moment, what we consciously choose to do and not what we feel we are doing forced by circumstances. Productivity means adopting an attitude for continued improvement.

2.4 Basic Types of productivity:

1. Partial Productivity

Partial productivity is the ratio of output to one variety of input, for example, labour productivity (ratio between output and labour cost). Similarly capital productivity (ratio between output and capital input) and material productivity (ratio of output to Material input).

2. Total Factor productivity:

Total-factor productivity is the ratio of net output to the sum of labour input and capital input. By net-output we mean total output minus intermediate goods and services purchased.

3. Total productivity:

Total productivity is the ratio of total output to the sum of all input factors.

In all the above definitions, both the output and input are expresses in 'real' or 'physical' terms by being reduced to Rupees of a base year.

We will see a simple example to explain the above three basic types.

Egg:- output = 10,000/-

Human Input = 3,000/-

Or labour Input = 2,000/-

Material Input = 3,000/-

Capital Input = 1,000/-

Other expenses Input = 500/-

And it is be assumed that these values are in rupees with respect to a base period.

Partial productivities:

Labour or human productivity = $Output Human\ Input$ = 100003000 = 3.33

Material productivity = $Output Material\ Input$ = 100002000 = 5

Capital productivity = $Output Capital\ Input$ = 100003000 = 3.33

Energy productivity = $Output \over Energy\ Input$ = $10000 \over 1000$ = 10

Other Expenses productivity = $Output \over Other\ expenses\ Input$ = $10000 \over 500$ = 20

Total factor productivity

$$= {Net\ Output \over Labour\ input + Capital\ input}$$
$$= {Total\ Output - Materials\ and\ services\ purchased \over Labour\ input + Capital\ input}$$

Assume that the company purchases all its materials and services including energy, machinery and equipment (on else) and other services such as marketing advertising, information processing, consulting et c., Then

$$= {10000 - 2000\ +3000 + 1000 + 5000 \over 3000 + 3000} = {3500 \over 6000} = 0.583$$

Total Productivity = $Total\ Output \over Total\ Input$

$$= {10000 \over 3000 + 2000 + 3000 + 1000 + 500} = {10000 \over 9500} = 1.053$$

2.5 Benefits of higher productivity in organizations

(1) Higher productivity in a company with respect to human and other physical resources means higher profits because the cost is reduced and

Profit = Revenue - Cost

(2) Higher productivity of a company leads to higher earning all its employees as more wages or production bonus will be paid.

(3) Continuous higher productivity may make the managers to reduce the selling price so that sales and production increases and consumers get the production at cheaper rate.

(4) The Government gets more revenue in the form taxes due to more profits earned by the companies with higher productivity.

(5) Exporters will be in a better position to compete in the international market to get more foreign exchange, because of reduction in prices with higher productivity.

(6) Higher productivity firms will be considered as guide to follow by the less efficient firms in the industry.

(7) Higher productivity in a firm contributes to increase in average standard of living

2.6 Measurement of Labour Productivity

Labour productivity is the ratio between the output and the labour cost. When the word productivity is used without a qualification as additional term, it is deemed or assumed as the labour productivity.

In general productivity is measured in terms of certain data. The labour productivity is measured in terms of physical output per man-hour.

When the ultimate product is identical and uniform throughout, the mere addition of all the numbers of items produced during a given time period. Egg:- One year, will give us the total number of units produced. This figure when divided by the labour input i.e., Man-hours total will give the physical output per man-hour.

In the plants or organizations where the final products are varied and not uniform, the physical out output can be converted into standard hours. The total of all the standard hours discharged in the production of all the outputs gives us the total standard hours. These total standard hours when divided by the actual Man-hours, it gives us another gauge for measuring labour productivity.

2.7 Capital productivity Measurement

Capital productivity is the measure of how well physical capital is used in providing goods and services. Productive use of physical capital and labor are the two most important sources of a nation's material standard of living.

OECD calculates capital productivity as the 'ratio between the volume of output, measured as GDP, and the volume of capital input, defined as the flow of productive services that capital delivers to production, i.e. capital services'.

Productivity measures are metrics that track your team's efficiency in accomplishing their tasks. They can help you manage your team's performance and figure out where everyone can improve. Productivity measures compare the resources – time, tools, energy – your team uses to the amount of work they do

The 3 Best Methods to Measure Employee Productivity:

Method 1: Management by Objectives.

Method 2: Measuring Quantitative Productivity.

Method 3: Measuring Productivity by Profit.

Establish a Baseline.

Define and Measure Tasks (Not Hours)

Set Clear Objectives and Goals.

Carry Out a Client Survey to Getting Insight

2.8 Management productivity

1) Slack

Chat and instant messaging have been around for decades, but Slack has seized the crown as the king of asynchronous communication. With desktop and mobile apps, typing out a quick message, or sharing a file with colleagues has never been easier.

2) Chanty · Project/Task Management

Chanty is another team chat option with desktop and mobile apps. It places a greater emphasis on ongoing conversations on particular topics, although one-to-one chats are also available. There's also the option to switch to audio or video chats.

3. Trello

The Kanban board king makes it a snap to keep tasks organized based on their category or status. It's also a breeze to pass the baton to others on the same Trello board when the project is ready for the next phase.

4) Proof Hub

Proof Hub is a one-stop-shop for project planning and collaboration. Keep projects organized on Kanban boards and Gantt charts, assign tasks, manage resources, track timesheets, and document it all on this platform.

5) Todoist

We all gotta do what we gotta do. With Todoist, our gotta do items stay organized and sorted according to their due dates, as not all to-do list items are created equal. Track your progress, hand off tasks to others, and manage recurring items from the palm of your hand (or on your desktop.

6) Shift

Streamline your workflow and aggregate all your email and social accounts in one spot with Shift. Never miss a message, an appointment, or a task while staying focused on the stuff you care about.

7) Economic Lot Size

Mathematical formulas which tell what volume of production should be done in one

single lot in order minimize the set-up costs, inventory coat and machine time etc.

8) Equipment utilization reports

Regular daily, weekly or monthly reports, that machine in (working) and out (out of

order) of service and compare this output with capacity. I.e., it shows the percentage of

utilization of the equipment per day or a week or a month.

9) Flexible Budgeting

Flexible budget sets expenses for standard levels of output. It tells what cost should be for the actual levels of output and how cost can change when output changes. I. e., the flexible budget can be adjusted according to the actual output volume and we can take that adjusted budget as the expected thing for comparison with the actual costs.

10) Flow process chart

Flow process charts are the charts showing the sequence of activities (operation, Inspection, transportation, delay and storage) by using symbols, which occur during a process or a procedure. We will be seeing this in detail in the method study chapter.

11) Forms Control

Integrated control over issue of data collected forms and reports in order to reduce their proliferation and to increase this usefulness.

12) Gnat Chart

Gnat Chart is a planning or a progress chart on which anticipated and actual performance is plotted against a horizontal time scale.

13) Indirect labour controls

indirect labour controls are the prescribed ratios of indirect to direct labour for specific operations used to help in allocating manpower.

14) Line of Balance

Line of balance is a control procedure for collecting measuring and presenting facts relating to time, cost and accomplishment – all compared with a specific plan.

15) Linear programming

Linear programming is a mathematical method and an operations research technique for finding best way of using the limited resources to get optimum output.

16) Memo Motion Study

In Memo Motion Study, films are taken at very low speeds which shows wasted time in long or irregular cycles while analyzing. (Egg:- achieving in front of tock room).

17) Motion Economy

Application of 22 principles developed by gilbert which form basis for improving use if human body, arrangement of work place and design of equipment.

18) Operations Analysis

Break down and study of each of time job factor's purpose, operations performed, inspection, material handling, material.

19) Performance standards

Performance standards are the periodic goals set for managers that are pinpointed so as to control cost scrap reduction and schedule compliance.

20) Power cost analysis

Power cost analysis is the study of utility bills, meter readings etc. for electricity, fuels, air-water usages.

21) Preventive Maintenance

Preventive maintenance is a technique of periodic inspection and overhaul of the machines so as to minimize machine break down time and loss of labour cost due to machine break downs and make best use of maintenance effort.

22) Replacement Studies

Systematic ways (such as rate of return, present worth et) to compute true or comparative value of capital investment.

This helps in deciding whether to replace the machinery or not.

23) Standardization

In order to increase the productivity by reducing the cost and investment the items or products will be standardized. i.e., in place of many types of screws, we will standardize the size of the screws into one or two or more so that the volume of inventory decreases, the investment tied up decreases and the cost of the items also decreases as they are standard items. (For this purpose, we have to decide whether the standardized sizes are suitable in all the situations where we are previously using the screws which are considered for standardization).

24) Value Analysis

A study of ever part or process to determine how much of its costs could be reduced without affecting its function.

25) Wages incentives

Bonuses paid to more productive workers, under controlled conditions, to

Cut manufacturing costs decisively.

26) Work Measurement

Measurement of time (by stop watch or predetermined methods) by individuals to perform tasks in order to identify and establish the standard time. This will be seen in the time study chapter in detail.

27) Work Sampling

Work sampling is the in-expansible method (cost is less) of random sampling (testing here and there which are selected randomly). To gather accurate facts about manpower or machine use.

28) Work Simplification

Work simplification is an organized commonsense act on the way the work is done, changes thinking habits, about what is accepted and useful work. By this the work will be simplified in such a way that un useful part is removed.

29) XR Control Chart

XR Control chart is statistical quality control technique for anticipating, in order to avoid defects and minimizing inspection.

2.9 Summary

The basic requirements for a human being in order to have a minimum decent standard of living are the minimum needed food, clothing, shelter, security and Essential services. The average standard of living can be increased in two main ways, i.e., increasing employment and/or increasing productivity which in turn increases the total goods and services produced in a country which leads to increase in average standard of living. The general definition for productivity is "The ratio of output to Input". The increase in production need not lead to a similar increase or an increase in productivity. Both are different. An increase in production may some time lead to decrease in productivity also if proper use of resources is not made.

There are three basic types of productivity. They are (a) partial productivity which is ratio between output to one variety of input. Egg:- labour productivity (b) Total-factor productivity which is the ratio of net output (i.e., Total output minus intermediate goods and services purchased) to the sum of labour input and capital input. (c) Total productivity is the ratio of total output to the sum of all input factors. In all the above types of productivities both the inputs and outputs are expressed in real or physical teems by being reduced to rupees of a base year. There are lot of advantages for higher productivity which in total leads to an increase of average standard of living.

Managerial productivity in getting more attention in order to get benefits of total productivity. Managerial productivity is the ratio value added (to the output by the management) and the total salaries of management.

There are lot of ways to increase the productivity.

2.10 Glossary

Capital productivity: It is one type of partial productivity. It is ratio between and capital input. In the ratio, normally in the place of capital input the working capital employed will take.

Labour productivity: It is one type of partial productivity. It is the ratio between output and lab our input.

Management productivity: It is the ratio between the value added by the management and the total salaries of management.

Net output: It is equal to total output minus intermediate goods and services purchased.

Partial productivity: It is ratio of output to one variety of output. Examples are labor productivity, capital productivity, Material productivity etc.,

Productivity: It is ratio of output to input.

Standard of living: It is the degree of material well-being necessary for sustaining and enjoying life.

Total-factor productivity: It is the ratio of net output to the sum of labour input and capital input.

Total productivity: It is the ratio of total output to the sum of all input factors.

2.11 Reference Books

International labour office, Geneva, Introduction of work study, universal Book corporation, Bombay, third (revised) Edition. Pages 3 to 16

K.C. Jain and L.N. Aggarwal, production planning control and Industrial management, Khanna Publishers, Delhi First Edition. 595 to 609.

David Sumanth, Productivity engineering and Management, MC Glow-Hill Book company pages 3 to 7, 76 to 228, 303 – 329.

2.12 Self-assessment

1) The standard of living of a representative person or family widely varies from country to country (Yes/No)

2) The standard of living can change or vary from community to community within a country (Yes/No)

3) Enough food, clothing and shelter are the only basic requirements for a person to have a decent standard of living (Yes/No)

4) Increase in productivity leads to increase in average standard of living of a community/country (Yes/No)

5) Productivity is the ratio of ___________________ to ________________

6) Labour productivity is a type of partial productivity (Yes/No)

7) Total productivity is the ratio of _____________ to _____________

8) Management productivity is the ratio of _____________ to _____________

9) Brain storming is one of the ways of increasing productivity (Yes/No)

10) Work measurement is one of the ways of increasing productivity (Yes/No)

ANSWERS:

1. Yes 2. Yes 3. No 4. Yes 5. Output, input 6. Yes 7. Total output, Total Input 8.Value added by management, total salaries of managers 9. Yes 10. Yes

2.13 Discussion and project work

Discuss with your friends whether productivity is good for all or not. Gather information from a company balance-sheets for 3 or 4 years, calculate and find whether productivity increased or decreased.

2.14 Questions

1) What is productivity? How it effects Standard of living?

2) What are the objectives of productivity?

3) What is labour productivity? How it is Measured?

4) What is management productivity? Briefly explain?

5) Briefly explain 7 Methods of increasing productivity?

CHAPTER THREE

Work Study – Method Study

Work Study – Method Study

The objectives of 'Work Study – Method Study' chapter is to make the student understand –

(a) The meaning of work study and method study

(b) The history of work study and method study

(c) The relationship to productivity

(d) The process of method study in detail with main concentration on the recording techniques of the facts related to the work selected for the study.

(e) Objectives of work study and method study.

CONTENTS

3.1 Introduction

3.2 Work Study: a direct means of raising productivity

3.3 Relationship between techniques of work study

3.4 Basic procedure of work study

3.5 Method study definition and objectives

3.6 Basic procedure of method study

3.7 Selection of the work to be studied

3.8 Recording the facts

3.9 Examine the facts critically

3.10 Develop the improved method

3.11 Defining the improved method

3.12 Installing the improved method

3.13 Maintaining the new method

3.14 Motion study

3.15 Summary

3.16 Glossary

3.17 Reference Books

3.18 Self-assessment

3.19 Project work

3.20 Questions

3.1 Introduction

"Work-study is a generic term for those techniques, particularly method study and Work Measurement, which are used in the examination of human work in all its contexts, and which lead systematically to the investigations of all the factors which affect the efficiency and economy of the situation being reviewed, in order effect improvement".

From the above definition, it is clear that Work Study aims at increase productivity i.e., Increasing the amount of output produced from a given quantity of inputs. It needs little or no further capital investment.

Work stud was widely known from a long time as 'Time and Motion Study'. The terms Time study and Motion Study had many interpretations since their origin. Time study which was originated by F.W. Taylor had major concentration on Time Standards determination. Motion improve study which was developed by Geberth's was employed largely for improving the methods. After 1930, a general movement started to study the work with an objective of finding better and simpler methods of doing the work. Then they started thinking of a combined effort of 'Time and Motion Study'. today the scope of Time and Motion Study is much broader, and the practices have changed from the previously used ones. We are now concerned with the design of work systems and methods. Presently our objective is to find the ideal method or near ideal method, that can be practically used, where as in the past, the emphasis was too often on improving existing methods. Because of these things some feel that 'Time and Motion Study' is too narrow and insufficiently descriptive than the new term 'Work Study'.

3.2 Work Study: a direct means of raising productivity:

One of the effective ways of raising productivity in the long run, is the development of new process and installation of more modern plant and equipment. But this requires heavy capital investment. Work Study on other hand aims at approaching the problem of increasing productivity through the systematic analysis of existing operations, processes and work methods with a to increase their efficiency. Work Study therefore increases productivity with little or no extra capital expenditure.

The complete effect is felt in an organization only when work study is applied everywhere, and when everyone feels intolerance of waste in any form, whether of material, time, effort if human ability which is the basis for success of work study.

3.3 Relationship between Techniques of Work Study

In the definition, it was indicated that the term Work Study, includes several techniques, but in Practical Method Study and Work Measurement.

"Work Measurement is the application of Techniques designed to establish the time for a qualified worker to carry out a specified job at a defined level of performance".

In simple, we can say that Method Study, and Work Measurement are closely linked. The Method Study is concerned with the reduction of work content of a job time associated with it and establishment of time standards for the operations which are performed according to the improved fashion determined by Method Study. The relationship can be shown diagrammatically as follows:

3.4 Basic Procedure of Work Study

The following is the basic procedure of work study which applies to every study, whatever the operation or process being examined, in whatever the industry. This is the fundamental procedure and there is no short cut.

Steps involved in the procedure are:-

Work Measurement

To determine the Time Standards for performing the job

Work Study

Higher productivity is the outcome

Method Study

To simplify the job and find best and easy way of doing it.

(1) Select the job or process to be studied.

(2) Record everything that happens through direct observation with the help of best suitable recording techniques, so that the data is in the most convenient form.

(3) Examine the recorded facts critically and challenge everything that is done by questioning (a) The purpose of activity (b) The place where it is performed (c) The sequence in which it is done (d) The person who is doing it and (e) The means by which it is done.

(4) Develop the best method which is most economic by taking all the circumstances into consideration.

(5) Measure the quantity of work involved in the above selected method and calculate a standard time for doing it.

(6) Define the new Method and related Standard time so that it can always be identified.

(7) Install the new method as agree Standard Practice with the time allowed.

(8) Maintain the New Method by proper control procedures.

First three steps are there in Method Study and Work Measurement. Step five is the part of work measurement.

3.5 Method Study definition and objectives

The definition is given previously under the sub-heading "Relationship between techniques of work Study". The term Method Study is increasingly used in the place of motion study although it covers the same. American Society of Mechanical Engineers has given separate definitions for Method Study and Motion Study. The Motion Study being confined to hand and eye movement at the work place. However, Motion Study is sometimes used in text books with the same meaning as Method Study.

The objectives of Method Study are –

(1) The improvement of processes and procedures

(2) The improvement of factory, shop and work place layout and of the design of plant and equipment.

(3) Economizing the human effort and reduction of unnecessary fatigue

(4) Improvement in the use of materials, machines and man power

(5) The development of a better physical working environment.

There are a number of method study techniques suitable for tackling work study problems on which all scales from the layout of complete factory to the smallest movements of workers on repetitive work. In every case, however, the method of procedure is basically the same and there is no short cut route.

3.6 Basic Procedure or Method Study

We have already seen the basic procedure for the complete work study which covers the procedures of both Method Study and Time Study. Now, let us see the basic procedures of both Method Study and Time Study. Now, let us see the basic procedure for Method Study. The steps are as follows:

1. Select the work to be studied

2. Record the relevant facts about the present method by direct observation.

3. Examine those facts critically and in ordered sequence, using the techniques best suited to the purpose.

4. Develop the most practical, economic and effective method, having due regard to all contingent circumstances.

5. Define the New Method so that it can be always identified

6. Install that method as Standard practice.

7. Maintain that standard practice by regular routine checks

By the above simple steps do not try to feel that Method Study is easy and unimportant. On the other hand, Method Study may be very complex certain times. For the purpose easy understanding it has been reduced to these for few simple steps. Now we will see each step-in detail.

3.7 Selection of the work to be studied

The following are the factors that are to be kept in mind while selecting the work for the study

a. Economic considerations

Comparing the costs and benefits in order to decide whether the study is worth considering

a. Technical considerations

Make sure that the needed technical knowledge is available

c. Human Reactions

The mental and emotional reactions of the people who are going to be affected by the study are to be considered. If they are positive, study can be done. If not even through it is economical, it is better not to go for the study.

3.8 Recording the facts

The success of the complete procedure of the study depends on the accuracy with which the facts are recorded, because they act as basis for critical examination and the development of the improved method. So, recording should be clear and concise.

The general way of recording the facts is to observe and write. But in case of complicated processes which are common in modern organizations it is not suited. In certain cases, every minute detail is to recorded exactly. So even for very simple works we may have several pages of written information.

To overcome this difficulty other techniques are CHART and DIAGRAMS.

A. CHART indicating process sequence

1. Outline process chart

2. Flow process chart – Man type

3. Flow process Chart – Material type

4. Flow process chart – Equipment type

5. Two – handed process chart

B. CHART using a Time scale

1. Multiple activity chart

2. Simo chart

C. DIAGRAMS indicating movement

1. String diagram

2. Flow diagram

3. Cycle graph

4. Chrono cycle graph

5. Travel chart

A. CHARTS indicating process sequence (or) process charts. i.e., Representation of a series of event or happenings in the order of occurrence. In the process charts the following symbols used.

Operation

It indicates the main steps in the process, usually the part (charging the shape), material (adding or subtracting) or product concerned is modified or changed during the operation.

Inspection

It indicates an inspection for quality or check for quantity or both

Transport

IT indicates the movement of workers, material or equipment from place to place.

Temporary storage or delay

It indicates either a delay in waiting for next operation or kept aside temporarily without record until required.

Permanent storage or delay

It indicates the storage of objects which can be had in future only with some authorization.

In order to show the combined activities, the symbols are combined and shown, which means that both are performed at one time or at some work station by same operative.

Egg:- Operation and Inspection at one time

A1 Outline process chart

Outline process chart is a process chart giving an overall picture by recording in sequence only the main operations and inspections. In this chart we will not consider who has done it and where they have performed. This chart uses only the symbol and the time allowed for it (if known) is also added.

The advantages of outline process chart are –

i.   It presents a bird's eye view of the entire process

ii. Determines the requirements for detailed recording

iii. Establishing logical sequence of activities in process like assembly lines

iv. Selecting key operations for critical examination
v. These charts are often used in assisting the layout of a plant or during a product design where complete investigation by method study can point out wasteful material or even saving in machine tool.

Eg:- Watering the garden
Attach the pipe to the tap
Open the tap
Water the garden
Inspect whether every place is watered or not
Close the tap after watering the complete garden
Remove the pipe from the tap
Flow Process Chart:
A flow process chart is a process chart setting out the sequence of the flow of a product or a procedure by recording all events under study by using the symbols. In this flow process chart, in addition to operation and inspection symbols other three i.e., transport, delay and storage symbols are also used.

Egg:- Received, Check the number of pieces in the case and store.
Case lifted from truck and placed on inched truck
Slid on inclined plane
Placed on the hand truck
Moved to the packing place
Removed the lid/cover
Moved on to the receiving bench
Wait for unloading
Items removed from the case and kept on the receiving bench
Each item is inspected
Items placed in the case after inspection and lid is placed
Waiting for transport laborer's
Case transferred to stores
Case stored in stores.
Types of flow process chart
A2 Flow process chart – Man type
This type of chart records what the worker does.
A3 Flow process chart – Material type
This type of chart records what happens to material
A4 Flow process chart – Equipment type
This type of chart records how the equipment is used.
The above three flow process charts have the active voice in the man type and passive voice in other two. It can be clear by seeing the following examples.
Flow Process Charts
Man, Type Material Type
Drills castings Casting Drilled
Carried to bench Carried to bench
Picks up bolt (bolt) picked up
Inspects for finish finish inspected
A5 Two handed process chart
A two-handed process chart records the activities of both the hands of an operator. It is suited best for repetitive tasks of short duration only. Such a task is usually performed within the confines of a work place. The symbols used are same as process chart symbols except for storage which does not occur but used when a hand is used as a grip or

a vice to hold an object.

The chart will have two parallel charts each showing the activities of one hand. The two charts are synchronized in space to facilities the presentation of inter-related activities.

Egg:- Sorting the proper into dozens

Left hand Right hand

Wait for right hand reach to paper

Pick up the paper

Hold paper pass towards left hand

Place in left hand

Repeat for 12 times

(total)

Adjust the 12 papers Adjust the 12 papers

with the help of two hands with the help of two hands

Hold the papers, Fold the papers

Move folded papers to the tray

Place in the tray

Repeat the complete process until needed times.

B1 Multiple Activity Chart

Activity chart shows a breakdown of the process or of a series of operations plotted against time scale.

A multiple activity chart is a chart on which the activities of more than one subject (worker, machine or item of equipment) are each recorded on a common time scale to show their inter-relationship.

In this chart we use separate vertical columns, or bars to represent activities of different persons or machines against a common time scale. Study of this chart helps in rearranging these activities so that much of the ineffective or idle time is reduced.

It is useful for analyzing maintenance work, jobs involving people working in gangs and operations where the work is unbalanced and where there is unnecessary idle time.

Multiple Activity Chart

(Man, Machine Chart)

Activity: Machining of roller pins

Man Machine

Sl. No.

Description of activity

Symbol

Time Scale (Min.)

Symbol

Description of activity

1

Setting of Tool on Capstone

0.20

0.25

Idle

2

Feeding base stock

0.40

0.50

Idle

3

Idle

1.20

1.35

Turning the chromates of the pin

4

Pasting off

(Manual feed)

2.00

Machine working to part off component

The main uses of multiple activity chart are

(1) To eliminate or minimize the ineffective time of men r machines or both

(2) It enables complex processes to be recorded in a simple way for analysis

B2 Simo Chart

Simo chart is short form of simultaneous motion cycle chart which is one of the important recording techniques of micro motion study.

Micromotion study us worth doing in certain types of operations and particularly those with very short cycles which are repeated thousands of times. Examples are packing of sweets into boxes or food cans into cartons etc. This technique frequently uses the films. The major benefits of this are the person can perform repeatedly with minimum effort and fatigue.

These micro motion techniques (e.g., Simo chart) is based on the idea of dividing human activity into divisions of movements or groups of movements (knowns as Therbligs) according to the purpose for which they are made.

A Simo chart is a chart, often based on film analysis, used to record simultaneously on a common time scale. The Therbligs or groups of Therbligs performed by different parts of the body of one or more workers.

Simo chart is the micro motion form of the man type flow process chart. As it is used for short duration operations, first film is to be taken and it is to be screened in slow motion or stopped at any point to record it. For recording a list of Therbligs (like search, find select, grasp etc.) is given with symbols or Abbreviation or colors.

C1 String Diagram

The String diagram us a scale plan or model on which a thread is used to trace and measure the path of workers, material or equipment during a specified sequence of events.

When a job involves a great deal of movement the lines of a flow diagram may become though and confusing. In this case a string diagram can be used, with the additional advantage that the distance covered can be calculated by measuring he length of string or thread used.

It helps mainly in designing the factors layout.

C2 Flow Diagram

The flow pross charts can be also represented in the form of diagram so that a greater impact can be made or it is easier for the study.

Egg: serving dinner in a small hospital ward.

C3 Cyclograph

The Cyclograph is a record of a path of movement usually traced by a continuous source of light on a photograph, preferably stereoscopic. The path of movement of a hand, for instance may be recorded on a photograph by asking the worker to wear a Ring carrying a small light which will make the trace on the photograph. Similarly, the movement of the worker can be recorded by a light on his helmet.

C4 Chrono cycle graph

The chrono cycle graph is a special form of cycle graph in which the light source is suitably interrupted so that the path appears as a series of pear-shaped dots, the pointed end indicating the direction of movement and the spacing indicting the speed of movement.

The above two i.e., cyclograph and chrono cycle graph are of limited application when compared to other techniques discussed here.

C5 Travel Chart

A travel chart is tabular record for presenting quantitative data about the movements of workers, materials or equipment between any number of places over any given period of time.

Travel chart is quicker and more manageable recording techniques when compared to string diagram where there are many movements along complex paths. In this case the string diagrams may look like a forbidding maze of crisscrossing lines.

3.9 Examine the facts critically

After recording the facts, we have to critically examine the facts. For this purpose, we have the questioning technique.

The questioning technique is the means by which the critical examination is conducted, each activity being subjected in turn to systematic and progressive series of questions.

Questioning technique examines

The PURPOSE for which

The PLACE at which

The SEQUENCE in which the activities are

The PERSON by whom undertaken

The MEANS by which

With a view to ELIMINATING

COMBINING Those

REARRANGING activities

Or SIMPLIFYING

The following is the list of questions that are to be asked for each activity.

Purpose : What is done?

Why is it done?

What else might be done?

What should be done?

Place : Where is it done?

Why is it done there?

Where else might it be done?

Where should it be done?

Sequence : When is it done?

Why is it done then?

When might it be done?

When should it be done?

Person : Why does it?

Why does that person?

Who else might do?

Who should do it?

Means : How is it done?

Why is it done that way?

How else might it be done?

How should it be done?

The above questions are to be asked in the same above sequence every time a method study is undertaken.

3.10 Develop the Improved method

After getting the answers for the above questions we can develop the best possible method. For this purpose, the proposed improved method should be compared with existing method so that we can make sure that no point is overlooked or left.

3.11 Defining the Improved method

For the jobs other than performed and virtually controlled by the machines, it is desirable to prepare a written standard practice also known as "operative instructions sheet".

3.12 Installing the improved method

Installing the new improved method is a very improvement stage as the management, workers, workers representatives should accept. Then after gaining their acceptance, the retraining of workers should be taken. Then have close supervision unit it is implemented completely and running as expected.

3.13 Maintaining the new method

After the method is installed, it should be maintained in its defined form and the workers should not be allowed to slip back into old methods or introduce elements/activities no allowed unless there is a very good reason for doing so.

3.14 Motion study

While defining the method study we made it clear that 'Motion Study' is sometimes used in text books with the same meaning as method study. this term, 'Motion Study' is getting replaced gradually by the term 'Method Study' even though it covers almost exactly the same field.

But any way, the difference is shown in the definitions of both the terms by American Society of Mechanical Engineers.

They defined the Motion Study as "Study confined to hand and eye movements at the work place".

Normally in the Motion Study techniques the film will be used. These are of mainly two types.

(a) Motion pictures at high speed with the of spring driven or motor driven cameras

(b) Memo Motion Photography: It is a form time lapse photography which records activity by the use of cine cameras adapted to picture at longer intervals than normal. The time intervals usually lie between ½ second and 4 second i.e., very low speed cameras. These films are normally used in Micro Motion Studies.

3.15 Summary

Work study is a new term used in the place of Time and Motion Study as it is broader and it means identification of ideal or near ideal method that can be practically used instead of just improving the existing method which was the aim of time and Motion Study. work Study is a direct means of raising productivity. It includes several techniques but in particular method study and work measurement. Method Study aims at performing the work by easier and more effective methods and reducing costs. The following are the steps involved in Method Study.

The first step deals with selection of the work to be studied. For third we have to think of cost benefit analysis, needed technical knowledge availability and the concerned people's reactions. The second step deals with the recording facts relating to the work. For this purpose, we have different charts and diagrams. Among these things the generally used ones are process charts and rarely used ones are cycle graph and chrono cycle graph. The third step is examining the facts critically. For this purpose, the best way is questioning. From the answers got in the above step we now think of next step i.e., developing the improved method. The next is defining the improved method. For this purpose, normally they prefer written standard practice also called operative instruction sheet. Last but one step is installing the improve method. Last but not the least step is maintaining the new method.

Motion study is the which is getting replaced by Method Study. But we can also have different meanings for both given by American study of mechanical engineers which says that Motion study deals with eye and body movements at the work place.

3.16 Glossary

Chrono cycle graph: A special form of cycle graph in which the light source is suitably interrupted so that the path appears as a series of pear-shaped dots. The pointed end indicating the direction of movement and the spacing indicating the speed of movement.

Cycle Graph: A record of path of movement usually traced a continuous source of light on a photograph, preferably stereoscopic.

Flow diagram: A diagram which shows the actual flow or movement so that a greater impact can be made and easier for study.

Flow process chart – Equipment Type: This type of flow process chart records how the equipment is used.

Flow process chart – Man Type: This type of flow process chart records what the worker does.

Flow process chart – Material Type: This type of flow process chart records what happens to material.

Method study: It is the systematic recording and critical examination of existing and proposed ways of doing work, as a means of developing and applying easier and more effective methods and reducing costs.

Micromotion study: It is study of every small movement in the operation selected for improvement. The selected operation will be normally of very short cycle times and which are repeated thousands of times.

Multiple activity chart: It is a chart on which the activities more than one subject (worker, machine or item if equipment) is recorded on a common time scale to show their inter-relationship.

Outline process chart: IT is process chart giving an overall picture by recording in sequence only the main operation and inspections.

Simo Chart: It is the short form of simultaneous motion cycle chart. It is a chart often based on film analysis used to record simultaneously on a common. Time scale, the Therbligs of groups of Therbligs performed by different parts of the body of one or more workers.

String diagram: It is a scale or model or which a thread is used to trace and measure the path of workers, materials or equipment during a specified sequence of events.

Therbligs: The human activity is divided into divisions of movements of groups of movements called therbligs.

Travel Chart: It is Tabular record for presenting quantitative data about the movements of workers, materials or equipment between any number of places over any given period of time.

Two – handed process chart: A process chart in which the activities of both the hands of an operator are recorded.

Work Measurement: It is the application of techniques designed to establish the time for a qualified worker to carry out a specified job at a defined level of performance.

Work Study: It is a generic term for those techniques, particularly method study and work measurement which are used in the examination of human work in all its contexts, and which lead systematically to the investigation of all the factors which affect the efficiency and economy of the situation being reviewed, in order to effect improvement.

3.17 Reference Books

International Labour Office, Geneva, Introduction to Work Study, Universal Book Corporation, Bombay. Third (revised) Edition, Pages 29 to 183.

Ralph M. Blanes, Motion and Time Study Design and Measurement of work, John Wiley and sons, Inc. U.S.A. Sixth edition, pages 3 to 31, 63 to 161, 169 to 189.

Cycasin and L.N.Aggarwal, Production planning control and industrial Management, Khanna Publishers, Delhi, Pages 610 to 718.

W. Grant Ireson and Engane L. Grant, Hand Book of Industrial Engineering and Management, Prentice-Hall of India Private Limited, New Delhi, 1971, pages 283 to 353.

3.18 Self-assessment questions

1. Work study is direct means of raising productivity (Yes/No)

2. Work Measurement aims at _________________

3. The improvement of processes and procedures is one of the objectives of _____________ study.

4. The first step in method study is _____________________

5. After selecting the work to be studied the next step is _____________________ in Method study procedure.

6. IF human reaction is not positive to study, but if it is economical, it is advisable to go for the study: (Yes/No)

7. In Outline process chart we use the symbols of operations, inspection, transport, delay and storage. (Yes/No)

8. Simo chart is one of the recording techniques of Micro motion study (Yes/No)

9. In order to develop and improved method questioning technique is used as a base (Yes/No)

10. Films can be used in analyzing the method/procedure (Yes/No).

Answers: 1. Yes 2. Establishing Time Standards for a qualified worker to carry out a specified job at a defined level of performance. 3. Method Study 4. Selection of work to be studied 5. Recording the facts 6. No 7. No 8. Yes 9. Yes 10. Yes

3.19 Project work

Normally fir certain function like marriage, opening ceremony etc., we go for invitation cards. After the printing we insert the cards into covers. Just fond or observe hoe it is being done. Then within the constraints of time, cost etc., select the recording technique and try to improve the method by reducing the unnecessary movements.

3.20 Questions

1. Give the definition and meaning of work study?

2. What is the objective of method study?

3. What is the basic procedure of Method Study?

4. What are the process charts?

5. What is multiple activity chart? Explain it?

6. What are flow diagram and string diagram?

7. After recording, analyzing the facts can be done by questioning method. Explain this method?

CHAPTER FOUR

Time Study

The objective of this chapter 'Time Study' are to make the reader understand.

(a) The meaning of work measurement and its objectives.

(b) Techniques of work measurement, mainly Time Study

(c) Finally, how a Time Study is to be conducted and the process of determining the Standard Time. i.e., in brief, the need and calculation or Standard Time.

CONTENTS

4.1 Work Measurement definition

4.2 Work Measurement objectives

4.3 Uses of Work Measurement

4.4 Work Measurement Techniques

4.5 Time Study definition and Meaning

4.6 Basic Time Study equipment

4.7 Steps in making the Time Study

4.8 Selecting the Job

4.9 Obtaining and recording information

4.10 Recording the complete description of the method

4.11 Breaking down the Job into elements

4.12 Sample size

4.13 Timing each element

4.14 Rating

4.15 Extending the observed times to Basic Times

4.16 Allowance to be made over and above the Basic Time

4.17 Calculation of Standard Time

4.18 Summary

4.19 Glossary

4.20 Reference Books

4.21 Self-assessment

4.22 Questions

4.1 Work Measurement definition

In the Work Study-Method Study chapter we mentioned that Method Study and Work Measurement are the main techniques of work study.

The definition of Work-Measurement is "The application of Techniques designed to establish the time for a qualified worker to carry out a specified job at a defined level of performance".

4.2 Work Measurement Objectives

a. It is means of measuring . the Time taken to perform an operation or a series of operations in such a way that the ineffective time is identified and separated.

b. In addition to identification of ineffective time, it is also used to set Standard Times for carrying out the work. So that, in future any ineffective time will not creep or enter: IF at all it enters, it will be shown as the excess of actual time over the standard time. This makes the Management alert .

4.3 Uses of Work Measurement

The Set Standard Time in Work Measurement can be used in

(a) Comparing the efficiency if alternative methods, when other conditions being equal, the method which takes least time is the best method.

(b) Ensuring that groups or teams are well balanced by each person having an equal amount of work to perform.

(c) Determining the number of machines an operator can operate by Man-Machine multiple activity charts.

(d) Planning and scheduling the production by well load fixing to men and machines, so that the resources are used to the best possible extent.

(e) Fixing selling price, promising delivery dates, estimation for tenders etc.

(f) Standard Cost determination.

(g) Helps in labour budgeting system.

4.4 Work Measurement techniques:

The following are the basic techniques by which Work Measurement is carried out

(a) Work Sampling

(b) Time Study

(c) Predetermined time Standards (PTS)

(d) Standard data.

4.5 Time Study definition and Meaning

Time Study is defined as a "Work Measurement Techniques for recording the times and rates of working for the elements of specified job carried out under specified conditions, and for analyzing the data so as to obtain the time necessary for carrying out the job at a defined level of performance".

Simply we can say Time Study is a technique of determining as accurately as possible from a limited number of observations. The Time necessary to carry out a given activity at a defined Standard of performance

4.6 Basic Time Study equipment

The following are the essential equipment in order to perform Time Study.

a) Stop Watch

b) Study Board

c) Time Study forms

In addition to the above, the following are also needed in the office of Time Study.

d) A small calculator

e) A reliable clock with a second's hand

f) Measuring instruments such as tape measure, Steel rule, micrometer, spring balance and tachometer (revolution counter). Other needed measuring instruments depending on the type of work selected for study.

a) Stop Watch

Two types of Stop Watches are in general use for Time Study. They are fly-back and non-fly back types.

Fly back type Stop Watch will have two buttons on it. One button is to be pressed either to start or to stop the watch. The second button is to be pressed to get the hands fly-back (go back) to the starting point (zero) without stopping the mechanism i.e., from the zero point they immediately move forward again, if we want to stop the watch and start it again from that stopped position first button is to be used to times.

So, by fly back type Stop Watches we can have individual timing (Using first and second buttons) or cumulative timing (using only first button.)

The non-fly back type we will have only one button. If we press the button for the first time it starts. If we press for the second time it stops. If we press for the third time hands go back to the zero position.

Any stop watch in general will have two hands with two dials each for one hand. The dials are divided depending upon the need.

b) Study board

Study board is simply a flat board, usually of plywood or of suitable plastic sheet on which Time study forms are to be placed. It is just like the exam pad used by the children which has a clip on the top. The study board may or may not have an extra fitting fix the stop watch. It should not too big or too small.

c) Time Study forms

The recording can be done on plain paper also. But it is suggested to have printed forms which contains the needed information regarding the study on the first page on all the sheets (first and continuation). The ruling is there. There is no single standard format: Depending upon the need we can have it or organization may have a standard format throughout its life for any Time Study.

Other equipment

In the place of stop-watch, other timing equipment can be used to have more accurate measurement of time. The two other equipment which are giving importance are -

a) Motion picture camera:

which runs at a constant speed and while recording the film is projected at an equal constant speed.

b) Time Study machine:

In this machine, marks are made on a paper tape which is running at a constant speed by pressing both the keys which it has. To stop one key is to be pressed. Its main advantage over stop watch is the observer can observe the operation continuously instead of looking at it and reading the Stop Watch. This helps mainly to record timing of very short elements. At the end the tape is to be measured.

4.7 Steps in making the time Study

1) Selecting the job for time Study

2) Obtaining and recording all the information available about the job, the operative and the surrounding conditions, which is likely to affect the carry out the work.

3) Recording a complete description of the method, breaking down the operation into elements.

4) Examine the detailed breakdown to ensure that the most effective method and motions are being used, and determine the sample size.

5) Measuring with a timing device (Usually a stopwatch) and recording the time taken by the operative to perform each 'element' of the operation.

6) At the same time, assessing the effective speed of working of the operative relative to the observer's concept of the rate corresponding to Standard rating

7) Expending the observed times to 'basic times'

8) Determining the allowances to be made over and above the basic time for the operation

9) Determining the 'Standard Time' for the operation. Now we see each step-in detail.

4.8 Selecting the job

A time study should not be made for an operation until a request from an authorized person is received. Usually, a foreman or a plant manager or a chief engineer or a production control supervisor or a cost accountant etc., who needs time study, will make such a request.

The following are some of the reasons for making such a request

a) The job is a new one, i.e., not previously carried out (new product, component, operation or set of activities)

b) A change in material or method of working has been made which needs a new time standard

c) A complaint received from a worker or workers leader about the time Standard for an operation.

d) Standard Time is required for a new incentive scheme.

e) The cost of particular job appears to be excessive etc.

After receiving the request for a time Study, we have to check whether the Method Study has been undertaken. This is because if the present method is not the best method after time Standard is fixed, method may be changed which needs an adjustment in Time Standard again. Then if the job is suitable for Time Study, we can go for next step.

4.9 Obtaining and recording information

We have to get and record all the information available about the job, the operative and he surrounding conditions. In addition to this we have to gather the needed information i.e., the details of operation selected for Time Study, when it is conducted, how it is conducted, who has conducted, who has requested, where it has been done etc. regarding surrounding conditions it is better to take photograph.

This filling-in or all the information which is relevant is done through direct observation. It is needed in the case of future reference.

4.10 Recording the complete description of the method

Normally Method Study should be completed and implemented. So before actually starting the recording of times, we have to check whether the set standard pattern is being followed. After getting satisfied that the method which is standardized is being followed or a better method is followed, record the complete description of the method followed. It acts as check in future.

4.11 Breaking down the job into elements

Timing the complete job operation is seldom or rarely satisfactory. So, the job or operation is to be divided into elements and timings of each one is done is study which good.

Reasons for breaking the job into elements are –

(a) The operator may not work at the same tempo (speed) throughout the operation. By breaking up, we can use separate performance ratings for different elements depending upon the performance of operation.

(b) By breaking up, we can identify where the workers are using more time or less time and on what element. Normally workers tend to spend less time on inspection. This thing can be classified by breaking up which cannot be identified over-al study.

(c) By breaking up, we find standard times of each element. By combining all of them we can find the Total Standard time of the operation which is more accurate etc.

"An element is a distinct part of a specified job selected for convenience of observation, Measurement and analysis".

i.e., The element should be as short as possible but the timing should be accurately possible. The human element (work done by humans) should be separated from the machine elements. The constant elements should be separated from variable elements (here the constant and variable means the time is constant or variable when performed at different situations).

4.12 Sample size

The size of sample i.e., the number of readings that must be for watch elements is to be determined. While doing so we have considered the needed confidence level accuracy margin.

For this purpose, first we have to make a preliminary study with some small sample.

The following is the formula with 95.45 confidence level and margin of error of ±   5%.

n = 40ñ$\sum X2$- $\sum X2 \sum X$ 2

where n = preliminary study sample size

$\sum$ = sum of values

X = readings (values)

Let us see a small examples for this to make it further clear.

The preliminary study readings are 7, 6, 7, 7, 6.

Then X = 7 6 7 7 6 = 33 = $\sum$X

X2 = 49 36 49 48 36 = 219 = $\sum$X2

n = 5

n = 405(219)- 33233   2 = 8.81 or 9 readings.

So, the sample size needed is 9 items with a confidence level 95.45 and a margin of error of ±   5%.

After getting 9 sample readings if we apply the same above formula, we may need a bigger sample also. Continue this until is sufficient.

Some authors and companies have given a table of sample sizes required depending on cycle time.

Timing each element

After identifying the elements and the sample size we can start timing each element. The general method for recording the timings is by using stop watch. There are two principal methods with the Stop Watch i.e., cumulative timing and fly back timing.

In cumulative timing the watch is not stopped or returned to zero after every element. Just observe the watch and record the time. The time of any element is the difference between the end time and start time of that element.

In fly back timing the time for each element is directly recorded by getting the hands to zero after every element.

In general, cumulative timing is accepted than fly back timing.

4.14 Rating

Assessing the effective speed of working of the operative relative to the observer's concepts of the rate corresponding to Standard Rating, is the next step to be performed.

Rating which is nothing but the performance rating is the mental comparison by the Time Study observer between the actual performance of an operator under observation with his own idea of a standard performance for a given method.

The time study be conducted on the representative worker or average worker. But the exact average worker who represents the total group is difficult to find in reality. So, we need rating. The concept of rating is also important as workers do not work consistently throughout the day or week or month etc.

In order to compare the observed speed of working and standard speed in an effective way, it is needed to have a numerical scale. We have 100-133, 60-80 and 75-100 rating scales. 100, 60 and 75 denote Standard rate.

In 100-133 scale, 100 represents the Standard rate i.e., the normal rate of working of the motivated qualified worker. If the actual worker under observation is performing with less speed than the concept of Standard, rate him below 100. But if he is performing with more speed than rate above 100 but below 133.

To check the ratings given by the Time Study person, the following formula can be used.

Observed Time X Rating = A constant

4.15 Extending the observed times to Basic times

The observed times are to be extended to the basic time. Time basic time required to carry out the work at standard rating.

Basic Time = *Observed Time X Observed ratingStandard rating*

For egg: observed Time Observed Rating

(Decimal minutes)

(Each min = 100 parts)

0.20 100

0.16 125

0.25 80

Observed rating X Observed Time = A constant

0.20 X 100 = 20

0.16 X 125 = 20

0.25 X 80 = 20

Basic Time = *Observed Time X Observed ratingStandard rating*

= 0.25 X 80100   = 0.20 decimal min.

Note: 1) Normally rating to the nearest five is widely in practice.

2) Every element of activity, performed should be rated during its performance before the Time is recorded without having effect of next and before elements.

As we are doing rating before recording the actual time and rating is made as nearest to 5 multiples, we may get different basic times for every recording. Then find the average.

Egg:

Rating 80 85 90 95 100 105

Observed Times 31 31 30 28 26 24

30 30 28 27 25

30 29 27

Total basic times for each rating 48.8 77.35 78.3 77.9 51 25.2

So, Average basic time = 358.5514   = 25.16 = 26.

4.16 Allowance to be made over and above the basic time

In Time Study we fix the time needed for not only performing (standard performance) the actual job but also the time which is considered necessary for relaxation.

Total time fixed = Basic time + Relaxation + Any other

By time study as allowance related

Standard time allowance

Relaxation allowance:

Relaxation allowance is the allowance given as a person needs some rest time to recover from fatigue and some time to attend his personal need (washing, having a drink, going to nature's call).

Relaxation allowances are given as percentages of the basic time. They are normally calculated on an element – by – element basic (personal needs and basic fatigue, stand on both feet etc.) For this purpose, the standard tables are given.

The total of all the relaxation allowances of every element will give the relaxation allowance of a particular element (part of the job). General practices to allow a minimum of overall relaxation allowance of 10% for men and 12% for women of Basic Time.

Other allowances

It is sometimes necessary to incorporate allowances other than relaxation allowance in the calculation of standard time. They are –

(a) Contingency allowance:

Under certain conditions, it may be necessary to make a small allowance to cover irregular occurrences which are known to happen but whose incidence it may not be possible or economic to study.

It is also expressed as a % of basic time. Time contingency allowance should not be more than 5% and it should be given only when the time study person is absolutely satisfied.

(b) Policy allowance:

This is allowance given at the discretion of the management over and above other allowances. It is an increment other than bonus increment applied to Standard Time to provide a satisfactory level of earning for a specified level of performance under exceptional circumstances. This is not a part of time study. so, it should be dealt separately.

(c) Special allowances:

Special allowances may be given for any activity which are not normally part of the operation cycle but which are must for satisfactory performance of the work.

When Time Standards are used for payment determination it is necessary to give START-UP ALLOWANCE to compensate the time taken by any work or waiting time which necessarily occurs the start of the shift or work period or production run. Similarly, a SHUT-DOWN ALLOWANCE may be given for work or waiting time. That occurs at the end of the day. A CLEANING ALLOWANCE is to be given if the worker has cleaned the machine and work place time to time. TOOL ALLOWANCE is an allowance of time to cover the adjustments and maintenance of tools.

Like this depending upon the activity there can exist some other special allowances also.

4.17 Calculation of Standard Time

"Standard Time is the total time in which a job should be completed at standard performance".

After identifying the basic Time and allowances they are added up to get the standard time of each element. The sum of the standard times of all the elements of an activity or job gives the standard time of this activity or job.

The Standard time components can be shown as follows:

Observed Time Rating Factor Allowance

(If performance at a

greater speed than

standard)

Observed time

Basic Time

Standard Time

In a case where observed time is rated less than standard rate, the rating factor will be shown inside the observed time.

Let us see a small example in order to classify the calculation of standard time further.

Observed time = 8 minute

Rating Factor = 110%

Allowances = 5%

Then

Basic time = *Observed Time X RatingStandard rating*

= 8 X 110100   Standard rating is 100 as

rating is given as a

percentage

Basic time = 0.88 minutes

Then Standard time = Basic Time + Allowances

= 0.88 + 5100   X 0.88

= 0.924 minute

4.18 Summary

Work measurement is the application of techniques designed to establish the time for a qualified worker to carry out a specified job at a defined level of performance. The main objectives of work measurement are removal of ineffective time and acting as a check for future so that the ineffective time will not enter. There are many used like fixing the standard cost, selling price, preparing labour budget, comparing alternative methods when other things are same etc.

Time Study is one of the basic techniques of woke measurement. It is used to determine as accurately as accurately as possible from a limited number of observations, the time necessarily to carry out a given activity at a defined standard of performance. The main equipment needed ire used by Time study people is stop watch.

The following are the steps in Time Study to determine the Standard Time (a) select the job for Time Study (b) Obtaining and recording the needed information regarding the job, the operative, working conditions. (c) Record the complex description of the method after making sure that it is the best way of doing the job. (d) Then break the job into small elements (e) After this, we have to find or calculate the needed sample size. (f) Timing each element for required times (sample size) (g) Then rating is to be done for every observed timing before the timing is recorded. (h) Then extend the observed timings to basic timing. The formula is

Basic time = *Observed Time X Observed ratingStandard rating*

(I) Find the allowances that are to be allowed like relaxation allowance. All the allowances are expressed as a % of Basic Time (j) The last Step is to calculate the Standard Time which is expressed as

Standard = Basic Time + allowances

4.19 Glossary

Basic Time: Basic Time is the time required to carry out the work at standard rating calculated by

Observed Time X Observed RatingStandard rating

Element: An element is a district part of a specified job selected for convenience of observation, measurement and analysis.

Rating: Rating is nothing but performance rating which is the mental comparison by the time study observed between the actual performance of an operator under observation with his own idea of a standard performance for a given method.

Standard Time: Standard time is the total time in which a job should be completed at standard performance.

Time Study: Time study is a technique of determining as accurately as possible from a limited number of observations, the time necessarily to carry out a given activity at a defined standard or performance.

Work Measurement: It is the application of techniques designed to establish the time for a qualified worker to carry out a specified job at a defined level of performance.

4.20 Reference Books

1. International Labour Office, Geneva, Introduction to Work Study, Third (Revised)

Edition, Universal Book Corporation, Bombay, pages 187 to 271.

2. K.C. Jain and L.N. Aggarwal, production Planning Control and Industrial Management, Khanna Publishers, Delhi, First Edition, pages 718 to 729

3. Ralph Barnes, Motion a Time Study Design and Measurement of Work, John Wiley and Sons, U.S.A., Sixth Edition, Pages 342-417.

4. Elwood's S. Buffer, Modern Production/Operations Management, John Wiley and Sons, U.S.A.., Sixth Edition, pages 621 to 637.

4.21 Self-assessment

1. Difference Work Measurement and Time Study

2. Discuss the relevance of rating factor

3. Discuss the relevance and importance of Allowances

4.22 Questions

1. What is Time Study? What is the needed equipment for Time Study? Explain the stop watch working?

2. What is work measurement? What are the objectives of Work Measurement?

3. What are the steps in Time Study? Explain how a job is to be selected?

4. Explain the Allowances that are to be added to Basic time to get the standard time?

5. Explain the rating factor and the calculation of Basic Time?

CHAPTER FIVE

Application of Work Study Technique

The objectives of this 'Application of Work-Study Techniques' chapter is to make the student understand (a) The basic things that are to be satisfied before conducting the work study and (b) where and how Work-Study can be applied with the help of some examples.

CONTENTS

5.1 Good relations must be establishment before Work-Study is applied.

5.2 Work-Study and the Management

5.3 Work-Study and the Supervisor

5.4 Work-Study and the Worker

5.5 The Work-Study Man

5.6 General use of Work Study Techniques

5.7 Work Study in organisations

5.8 Some real examples

5.9 An example of most refined use of Motion and Time Study

5.10 An example of the simplest use of Motion and Time Study

5.11 An example of Method Study application

5.12 An example of Time Study application

5.13 Summary

5.14 Glossary

5.15 Reference Books

5.16 Self-assessment

5.17 Questions

The human factor is very important in the application of work study. to see its importance let us have a look at the following.

5.1 Good relations must be established before Work Study is applied

Work Study is not a substitute for good Management and never it can be. It is only one of the "Tools" in the hands of Managers. It will not change bad industrial relations good by itself. The Work Study aims at improving productivity. It is having to be enjoined, the relation between management and workers should be reasonably good before it is implemented.

i.e., Workers must have confidence in Managers on their sincerity towards (workers) them. It not, workers will think that Work Study is another trick played by the Management to extract more work from them without any extra payment or benefit.

Of course, in certain conditions like unemployment problem which is wide spread in the country, the work study can be imposed. In this case the workers will accept reluctantly.

So, we can say that good relations should exist between workers and management before the application of Work Study.

5.2 Work Study and the Management:

Management foreman and workers, generally speaking, are honest, hardworking people who perform their jobs as possible. But when a work study person comes and does some investigation, he may show or identify that the present methods (even though long practice) are having lot of wasteful time and effort. It won't mean that the Managers, workers and foremen are less clever or not working with full interest. It is generally because they were not trained of any operation or job which is done by Work Study.

If this is not made clear and the Work Study person is not tactful in handling the people, he may find that it is impossible to go further with his work as all of them may combine into groups and they will not allow him to do his job.

In order to have good results through application of Work Study, the help and acceptance from all the levels of management is required. Normally the bottom levels will try to follow the top levels. So, we have to gain the acceptance and a helping hand from the top first.

In order to get this, normally short courses regarding the Work Study will be held for the Top Management group i.e., managing Director, General Managers etc., If the Work Study person is able to show that he gained the acceptance of Top Management, the other levels of Management will start giving their helping had as their boss is doing.

5.3 Work Study and the Supervisor

The most difficult work of the Work Study person is to get the acceptance and the helping hand from the Supervisors. As lower-level Managers take their attitude from Top Managers, the workers will take their attitude from Top Managers, the workers will take their attitude from their immediate bosses i.e., Supervisors. If the Supervisors think "Work Study staff is nonsense" the workers will not respect or hear to the Work Study person to Specialist.

In order to get the acceptance and a helping hand from Supervisors, the Work Study specialist should do the following before the Work Study.

The whole purpose and the procedure of the Work Study should be carefully explained to the foreman or Supervisor, so that he understands exactly what is being done and why. This is to be done because the Supervisor or foreman may say no due to any one of the following reasons.

(a) The work he is supervising for many years is being challenge. The Work Study after implementation may improve the method, which may make the supervisor feel that he will be looked down by his bosses.

(b) Sometimes the Supervisor or foreman will be performing duties like planning the work, developing the method to follow, fixing rates, hiring and firing employees in many companies. Now by the Work Study introduction he may feel that his status or authority is reduced.

(c) IF disputes arise or workers are upset, he is the person who has to answer. So, it he is unable to understand the actual thing he will not be in a position to solve disputes or make workers satisfy.

The normal thinking of a supervisor or a foreman will be 'There is nothing to learn, from a person who has not spent much time as he has spent in the organization'.

In order to remove all the above misconceptions, the foreman or supervisor should be given some training regarding Work Study to prepare them to accept and give helping hand.

After the Work Study person or specialist has got acceptance, he has to follow certain norms.

(a) He should not give any order to workers directly. It should be given through Supervisor.

(b) He should not go to workers directly for the first time. He should be introduced to workers only by their boss.

(c) He should be careful so that the workers will not play with him. I. e., getting what they want through him (i.e., removing certain though element in the job etc.)

(d) He should not discuss any matter with the worker which is outside the area of work study. If the workers ask such questions, they should be referred to their supervisor or foreman etc.

5.4 Work Study and the Workers:

As stated earlier, if the worker has confidence in the sincerity of the Management, then there will be no difficulty in the application of Work Study. before performing work study all the problems must be discussed honestly. Before and while doing the work study the following things are to be kept in mind and followed. If we do so, the worker will have more positive attitude towards the Work Study.

(a) Management must take initiative for free and sufficient consultation before the Work Study is started.

(b) If Work Study is performed, the workers and their leaders are to be fully informed of all things that are being done. All the work study records must be made available to them so as to develop a feeling of confidence.

(c) Work Study finally aims at increasing the earnings of workers by improving the method which leads more profits/margins. This will be linked by workers. So, make it clear.

(d) There is may be strong resistance for change in the method by the workers. They must be explained about its advantages to the workers and the organization.

Still sometimes skilled workers may not be interested to change the method. Then it is better to leave them it their performance is reasonably satisfactory. The new improved method is taught to the new and young workers only.

(e) Sometimes workers hesitate in being timed, because it worried them as someone is standing nearby and observing.

The way out is seen that the work-study expert must see worker gets accustomed to his presence before he starts his recording.

(f) The workers leaders should be trained in the techniques of increasing productivity. This helps in understanding its importance and explain to their follow (other) workers. This will also ensure them that it will not harm them.

5.5 The Work Study Man:

The following are the qualities of a Work Study expert/person which are needed for

success.

(A) Qualification abilities

(I) Good knowledge of work study techniques

(ii) Good knowledge of different manufacturing process by which he is conducting the work study. this can be had by experience.

(iii) He must be well qualified. Normally an engineer or a management graduate is better off than any other person with low qualifications.

(B) Metal abilities

(I) Mentally prepared and interested to do that work

(ii) Good observation power i.e., Metal alertness, sharpness etc.

(iii) A man of clear thoughts

(iv) Power/ability to express things clearly

(C) Personal qualities

(I) Sincerity and honesty. This makes him to again confidence and respect of those with whom he has to deal.

(ii) Enthusiasm to work

(iii) Tactful in handling the situation

(iv) Self-confident, strong will power and courage

(v) Leadership capabilities

(vi) Good appearance

This is the back ground which is to be prepared of satisfied so as to start the Work Study. Before actually starting the Work Study it is better to think of working conditions and working environment. This is because it has effect on the productivity and performance.

5.6 General use of work study (Method and Time Study)

We should not think that work study can be applied only to the manufacturing operations. It can be even applied to medical field i.e., for operations conducted by a doctor or a doctor. This work study when applied to operations conducted by doctors, it will reduce the total time of the operation. When the total time of operation is reduced or the method of operation is improved, the probability of saving the life of the patient increases.

In Queuing theory (waiting the models) the basic assumption is service time and time between the arrivals can be found. Time study is the means to find these timings. The Queuing Theory will be seen in detail in one of the remaining chapters.

Like this, it can be applied to any activity or occupation like battle activities, hotel work, house work, cafeteria work, farm work, departmental store, storage or warehouse operation, heavy or light factory work etc., wherever the motion and time study approach fits.

5.7 Work-Study in organizations

Total Work Study is mainly applied in organization in order to increase productivity by increasing the output from the same input i.e., better utilization of resources with less or no extra capital.

5.8 Some Real Examples

The following are the few examples from few industries who have used these techniques and got much productivity increase or gain.

1. Tata Engineering and Locomotive Company: As a result of Method Study, layout changes and revised producer design, actual-man hours per boiler and per locomotive were brought down from 10,000 to 6,200 and from 42,000 to 27,000 respective.

2. Indian Telephone Industries: By detailed layout studies conducted and introduced into a produce department, it was possible to increase productivity by 15% with in the same floor space available.

3. Voltas: By improved methods of storage, proper layout and use of material handling equipment have enabled a release of about 9000 square feet in one of the gods owns, effecting a saving in rent of Rs. 18,000/- per annum.

Only a few examples are given here in order to explain how much productivity can be improved by using Method Study activities.

5.9 An example of most refined use of Motion and Time Study

The job is a semiautomatic lathe operation. The data for this operation are given
below.

(a) There are 100 employees who are performing this operation. They work 40 hours per week. (each)

(b) The job is a permanent one. The cycle time is 0.25 minute of which 60% is handling time and 40% is machine time.

(c) The special semiautomatic lathe, fully equipped with cost 30,000/- when purchased.

As 100 employees are there and they are working 40 hours each per week and cycle
time 0.25 minute.

Total Number of items produced in a week = 100 X 40 X 600.25
= 9,60,000 units
Then the number of items produced in a year = 9,60,000 X 52
(52 Weeks approximately) = about 50 million

As per the details given each item needs 0.25 minutes i.e., ¼ minute = 15 seconds. If we reduce by one second per item by work study techniques.

The new output per week = *Seconds available by labourersNo.of seconds needed per item*

= 100 X 40 X 60 X 6014
= 9,60,000 items.

The increase in output units per week itself is 68,571.4 items just by decreasing one second in the labour time per unit.

So, for such a situation we need to have a most refined motion and Time Study i.e., Micro Motion Study is advisable.

5.10 An example of the simplest use of motion and Time Study

The job is drilling and counter boring a small bracket on a sensitive drill press. The job requires one person for 10 days in month. The job I expected to last for 6 months. If for every hundredth of a minute saved per item, there would a saving 40/- per year in labour cost.

In this case, it is better than the work study person spends very less time i.e., few hours to analyze and improve the method.

5.11 An example of Method Study application

Eg: Activity is finish casting

Multiple Activity chart

(Man – Machine chart) Original Method

Man Machine

Activity

Symbol

Time

Scale

(min)

Symbol

Activity

Remove the finished casting cleans with compressed sir

0.2

Gauges depth on surface plate

0.4

Brakes sharp edge with file and clean with compressed oil

0.6

Cleans machine. With compressed oil

0.8

Locate casting in fixture. Start machine and auto feed.

1.0

Idle

1.2

Working

For

Finishing

The

casting

Multiple Activity Chart

(Man, Machine chart)

Improved Method

Activity

Symbol

Time Scale (min)

Symbol

Activity

Remove finished castings

0.1

Cleans machine with compressed air

0.3

Locate casting in fixture Start machine and auto feed.

0.5

Break sharp edge with file and clean with compressed air

0.7

Working for finishing the casting

Gauges depth on surface plate

0.9

Place in box. Obtain new Casting and places by machine

1.1

Idle

1.3

5.12 An example of time study application

Normally before going for Time Study, we have to check whether the Method Study has been done or not. This is needed because if Method may not be the best method. So, if we apply Time Study and fix standard time, in future it may need some adjustments which again demands for a change in standard time.

An activity observed for 30 Times and they are also rated as follows by the observed.

Rating: 80 85 90 95 100 105

Observed 31 32 30 28 28 27

Times (in Mins): 31 30 30 27

30 30 27 27

31 26 28 26

31 27 27 27

28 26 28

29 29 27

29

29

29

In the above, rating is done as % and Allowances 10%

Solution:

Now we have to calculate the Basic /time. As we have 30 observed times and ratings, we get 30 individual Basic Times. But what we need is (selected) one basic time which is nothing but a sample average.

Basic Time = *Observed Time X RatingStandard Rating*

The total of all the individual basic Times when each basic time is rounded is 797.

So selected basic time = 79730

= 26.57 minutes

Standard Time = Basic Time + Allowances

= 26.57 + 10100   X 26.57

= 26.57 + 2.567

= 29.227

= 29.23 minutes.

5.13 Summary

The human element is very important in the Work Study application. In order to see how it is important we have to see the following (a) good relations must be established between workers and management before the work study is taken. This is because it by itself can't change bad industrial relations into good. (b) The management particularly the top management should give acceptance and helping hand without which work study is useless. (c) The supervisor is very important to consider the Work Study as he is the person with whom the work study specialist has to work hand-in-hand to get the work done. (d) Finally, the acceptance is to be gained from the actual workers.

In order to perform the Work Study well there are certain qualities that are to be there in the work study specialist (Egg: qualification, experience, knowledge about Work Study techniques etc.)

Finally, after checking the above things, we can go for Work Study. But before actually doing it, it is better to consider and understand the working conditions and working environment as they have effect on the performance.

We should not think that work study is to be applied only to manufacturing organizations. It can be even applied operations conducted by doctor/doctors.

5.14 Glossary

Method Study: It is and systematic recording and critical examination of existing and proposed ways of doing work, as a means of developing and applying easier and more effective methods and reducing costs.

Multiple activity chart: It is a chart on which the activities of more than one subject (worker, machine or item of equipment) are each recorded on a common Time Scale to show their inter-relationship.

Time-Study: It is a work measurement technique for recording the times and rates of working for the elements of a specified job carried out under specified conditions, and for analyzing the data so as to obtain the time necessary for carrying out the job at a defined level of performance.

Work Study: Work Study is a generic Term for those techniques, particularly METHOD STUDY and WORK MEASUREMENT, which are used in the examination of human work in all its contexts the efficiency and economy of the situation being reviewed, order to effect improvement.

5.15 Reference Books

International Labour Office, Geneva, introduction of Work Study, Universal Book Corporation, Bombay, Third (Revised) Edition, pages 29-45, 79-373.

Ralph Barnes, Motion and Time Study Design and Measurement of Work, John Wiley and Sons Inc., U.S.A., Sixth Edition, Pages 32-99, 342-417.

Ralph Currier Davis, Industrial Organisation and Management, Halper & Brothers, New York, Third Edition, Pages 397-433.

T.R. Banga, N.K. Agarwal, S.C. Sharma, Industrial Engineering and Management Science, Khanna Publishers, Delhi, 1989, Pages 8-53.

5.16 Self-assessment

1) Why the Top Management acceptance is needed at fist to perform and have success of Work Study?

2) What is the need to have the supervisor's acceptance?

5.17 Questions

1) What are the qualities that a Work-Study expert should have?

2) Why the acceptance from management, Supervisors, Workers is needed to have work study implementation?

3) Work Study can be used not only for manufacturing processes Ut also for other activities like medicine (Operations), house works etc. Discuss.

CHAPTER SIX

MOTION ECONOMY

It is the purpose of this chapter to interpret some of the general rules or principles of motion economy which has been and are now being successfully used.

CONTENT

6.1 Introduction

6.2 Principles of Motion economy as related to the use of the Human body.

6.3 Principles of Motion economy as related to the arrangement of work place.

6.4 Principles of Motion Economy as related to the design of tools and equipment.

6.5 Summary

6.6 Glossary

6.7 References

6.8 Self-assessment

6.9 Questions

6.1 Introduction

Experience shows that the use of "check lists", "rules for fatigue reduction", and "principle of motion economy" can be helpful in work methods design. On several occasions Gilbreth listed certain "rules for motion economy and efficiency" which govern hand motions, and from time-to-time other investigators in this field have added to the list".

There is much yet to be done in determining the fundamental laws which permit the maximum amount of productive effort with a minimum of fatigue. Although the material in this chapters is discussed under the handing "principles of motion economy" it might perhaps have been more accurately designated as "some rules for motion economy and fatigue reduction".

Not all the principles presented in this chapter are of equal importance not does this discussion include all the factors which enter into the determination of better methods for doing work. These principles do, however form a basis a code or a body of rules-which, ire applied by one trained in the technique of motion study, will make it possible to increase greatly the output of manual labour with a minimum of fatigue.

These principles will be presented under the following three sub-division.

1. Principles of motion economy as related to the use of the human body

2. Principles of motion economy as related to the arrangement of the work place.

3. Principles of motion economy as related to the design to tools and equipment.

6.2 Principles of Motion Economy as Related to the use of the Human Body

1. The two hands should begin as well as complete their motions at the same time.

2. The two hands should not be idle at the same time except during rest periods.

3. Motions of arms should be made in opposite and symmetrical directions and should be made simultaneously.

It is obvious that in many kinds of work more can be accomplished by using both hands than by using one hand. For most people it is advantageous to arrange similar work on the left-and –right-hand sides of the work place, thus enabling the left and right hands to move together, each performing the same motions. The symmetrical movements of the arms tend to balance each other, reducing. The shock and jar on the body and enabling the worker to performs his task with less mental and physical effort. There is apparently less body strain when the hands move symmetrically than when they make non symmetrical motions, because of this matter of balance.

Ex: Filling Mailing Envelope with Advertising Material. This operation involved inserting four sheets of advertising material in a mailing envelope and tucking in the envelope flap. The job consisted of picking up the sheets one at a time with the right hand, transferring them to the left hand, jogging them, and then inserting them in the envelope. It is obvious that the left hand was idle part of the time, held the sheets part of the time, and worked in an in efficient manner during the rest of the cycle. Also, the right hand was idle part of the time.

Improved Method. Two small triangular pieces made from cardboard and tape were feast end to flat sheets of cardboard. The advertising material was stacked against the two sides of the triangular pieces, which served as fixtures, enabling the operator to pick up two sheets at a time with each hand. Rubber finger stalls facilitated the grasping. Since sheets of the particular size were mailed out at frequent intervals, the work place to handle this job was set up permanently. Triangular wood blocks are at A. The operation now consists of grasping two sheets of paper at a time with each hand, drawing them together, jogging them on block B, and inserting them I-the envelope.

When the operator used the old method of filling envelopes, picking up the sheets one at a time, her production was 350 per hour. Using the improved workplace layout and better method, she was able to fill 750 envelopes per hours. The new method is so much easier than the old that she has more than doubled her output.

4. Hand and body motion should be confined to the lowest classification with which it is possible to perform work satisfactorily.

The five general classes of hand motions are listed here because they emphasize that material and tools should be located as case as possible to the point of use, and that motions of the hands should be as short as the work permits.

General Classification of Hand Motions

1. Finger motions

2. Motions involving fingers and wrist

3. Motions involving fingers, wrist, and forearm

4. Motions involving fingers, wrist, forearm and upper arm

5. Motions involving fingers, wrist, forearm, upper arm and shoulder. This class necessitates disturbances of the posture.

5. Momentum should be employed to assist the worker wherever possible and it should be reduced to a minimum if it must be overcome by muscular effort.

In most kinds of factory work the total weight moved by the operator may consist of three components: the weight of the material moved, the weight of the tools or devices moved, and the weight of the part of the body moved. It is often possible to employ momentum of the hand, the material, or the tool to do useful work. When a forcible stroke is required to motions of the worker should be so arranged that the stroke is delivered when it reaches its greatest momentum.

6. Smooth continuous curved motions of the hands are preferable to straight line motions involving sudden and sharp changes in direction.

The simple operation of moving a pencil back and forth across a sheet of paper consists of two phases, the movement and the stop and change direction. Such abrupt changes in direction are not only time consuming but also fatiguing to the operator.

7. Ballistic movement are faster, easier, and more accurate than restricted (fixation) or "controlled" movements.

A ballistic stroke may terminals (1) by the contraction of the opposing muscles, (2) by an obstacle, or (3) by dissipation of the momentum of the movement, as in swinging a golf club.

It is not difficult to develop the free, loose easy movements of the wrist and forearm. The hand should move about the wrist for the shorter motions, and the forearm about the below for the longer motions. Experiments show that wrist and below movements are faster than finger or shoulder movements.

8. Work should be arranged to permit an easy and natural rhythm wherever possible.

Rhythm is essential to the smooth and automatic performance of an operation. Rhythm may be interpreted in two different ways. Perhaps is most frequently understood to mean the speed or the rapidly with which repeated motions are made. Reference is commonly made to the rhythm of walking or breathing. Rhythm may be interpreted in a second way.

The rapid movement through the area of velocity and the sudden feeling of strain and retarding at the end of this rapid movement constitute the bear. In consciousness they represent one event, and a series of such events connected in such a movement cycle maybe said provisionally to constitute a rhythm.

Individual Rhythm. Some have suggested that each individual has a "natural" rhythm or speed of movement that permits him to work with least effort. Some have urged that individuals should be permitted to work at this natural speed dandy that no outside force, such as a wage incentive, should be exerted to cause the individual to work faster than his natural rhythm. Since it seems difficult to determine what the natural rhythm is for any person and since most workers can be taught to change their rhythm in performing the same work (to work at different sets of motions), it seems that too much emphasis should not be place on this so-called natural rhythm.

Effect of Figure on Rhythm. In a study polishing in a silverware factory, it was found that during the morning the polishers worked at a uniform, rate and the units were finished at regular intervals. In the afternoon, however, the pressure used in holding the knife to the spoon against the polishing wheel increased, more strokes were used, and the time for polishing each piece was greater than in the morning when a regular rhythm was maintained. Fatigue, then, seems to break up the rhythm and disturb rhythm was maintained. Fatigue, then, seems to break up the rhythm ad disturb the coordination that makes for rapid and easy work. "The tried worker is, therefore, not only working slower than when she is fresh, but is also expending her energy extravagantly"

9. Eye fixation should be as few and as close together as possible.

Eye Movements. Although some kinds of work can be performed with little or no eye direction, where visual perception is required, it is desirable to arrange the task so that the eyes can direct the work effectively; that is the work place should be so aid out that the eye fixations are as few and as close together as possible.

6.3 Principles of Motion Economy as Related to the Work place:

10. There should be a definite and fixed place for all tools and materials.

Definite stations for materials and tools aid the worker in habit formation, permitting the rapid development of automaticity. It cannot be emphasized too strongly that it greatly to the worker's advantage to be able to perform the operation with the least conscious mental direction. There can be no virtue in requiring the worker to exert the unnecessary effort of deciding just what tool to pick up next or what part to assemble next, when by simply arranging the materials and tools properly, with a little practice the operator will automatically perform the work in the proper sequence, at a rapid rate, and with a minimum expenditure of effort.

When the eyes direct the hand in reaching for an object, the eyes ordinarily precede the hand. However, if materials or tools are located in a definite place and if they are always grasped from the same place, the hand automatically finds the right location and in many cases the eyes may be kept fixed on the point where the tools or materials are used.

11. Tools, materials, and controls should be located close to the point of use.

Very frequently the work place, such as a bench, machine desk, or table, is laid out with tools and materials in straight lines. This is incorrect, for a person naturally works in areas bounded by lines which are arcs of circles.

Normal Working Area Considering the horizontal plane, there is a very definite and limited area which the worker can use with a normal expenditure of effort. There is a normal working area for the right hand and for the left hand, working separately and for both hands working together. He normal working area for right hand is determined by an arc drawn with a sweep of the right and across the table. The forearm only is extended, and the upper arm hangs at the side of the body in a natural position until it tends to swing away as the hand moves toward the outer part of the work place. The normal working area for the left hand is determined in similar manner. The maximum working area for the right hand is determined by an are drawn with a sweep of the right hand across the table, with the arm pivoted at the right shoulder.

Arrangement of Machines. The following statement might be considered as a corollary to rule 11. In the continuous or progressive type of manufacturing machines apparatus, and equipment should be arranged so as to require the lease possible movement on the part of the operator.

12. Gravity feed bins and containers should be used to deliver material close to the point of use.

A bin with sloping bottom permits the material to be fed to the front by gravity and so relieves the operator of having to dip down into the container to grasp parts. Where many different parts are required, as in the assembly of an electric switch, it becomes necessary to nest the bins one above the other in order to have the material with in convenient reach of the operator.

13. Drop deliveries should be used wherever possible.

The work should be arranged so that the finished units may be disposed of by releasing them in the position in which they are completed, thus delivering them to their destination by gravity. This saves time. And moreover, the disposal of the objects by simply releasing them frees the two hands so that they may begin the next cycle simultaneously without breaking he rhythm.

14. Materials and tools should be located to permit the best sequence motions.

The material required at the beginning of a cycle should be placed next to the point of release of the finished piece in the preceding cycle. In the assembly of the bolt and washers the rubber washers in bins located next to the chute in to which the assemblies were disposed as the last motion of the previous cycle. This arrangement permitted the use of the two hands to best advantage at the beginning of the new cycle.

15. Provisions should be made for adequate conditions for seeing. Good illumination is the first requirement for satisfactory visual perception.

Visual perception may take place under such widely varying conditions that adequate provisions for seeing in one king of work are not always most suitable for another. For example, the provisions for seeing on such very fine work as watch making would be different from those recommended for inspecting "leather cloth" or tin plate for surface defects. However, if adequate illumination is provided, seeing is made easier in every case, although this may not be the complete solution of the problem. By adequate illumination is meant (1) light of sufficient intensity for the particular task, (2) light of the proper color and without glare, and (3) light coming from the right direction.

It should be borne in mind that the visibility of an object is determined by the following variables; brightness of the object, its contrast with its background, the size of the object, the time available for seeing, the distance of the object, the time available for seeing, the distance of the object from the eye, and other factors such as distractions, fatigue, reaction time, and glare. These variables are so related that a deficiency in one may be compensated by an augmentation of one or more of the others, provided all factors are above certain limiting values.

The intensity of illumination falling on an object and the reflection factor of the object or that of its background should be considered together in providing adequate illumination.

Use of special Spectacles for Very Fine work. On certain kinds of very find work the eye must be kept very near the object, however high the intensity of illumination may be. The constant use of the eyes of objects at such close range imposes a serious strain on the muscles of convergence and accommodation. Experiments show the special spectacles are advisable to permit the eyes to assume their normal condition. An increase in output approximating 12% has been found to result from the use of glasses on such work as mounting lamp filaments. "linking" in hosiery making and "drawing-in" in weaving processes.

Time for Seeing. Seeing can take place only after the eyes come to a stop and are focused on the object. In the object process of reading a printed page, for example, the eyes do not make a continuous movement along the line, but rather move in a series of jumps or leaps. The intensity of illumination affects the time required for seeing.

Inspection Work. The provision for adequate conditions for seeing is of paramount importance in inspection work, such work is usually highly repetitive, exacting in nature, and predominantly mental in its demands. Constant attention and almost continuous use of the eyes are required in many kinds of inspection work. Perception of a defect must be followed by instant action on the part of the inspector to reject the defective depart. Some individuals are able to see smaller differences than others and to perceive the same differences with greater speed. Since reaction time and visual acuity are important elements in most inspection work, it is essential that persons be selected by means of suitable tests before being employed for such work.

16. The height of the work place and the chair should preferably be arranged so the alternate sitting and standing at work are easily possible.

The worker should be permitted to vary his position by either sitting or standing as he prefers. Such an arrangement enables the individual to rest certain sets of muscles, and a change of position always tends to improve the circulation. Either sitting or standing for long periods of time produces more fatigue than alternately sitting or standing at will. In many kinds of work provision can easily be made for this sitting-standing combination.

Space between Top of Seat and Undersurface of Bench Top. The work place should be constructed to permit plenty of leg room for the worker. Braces, shafts, and other obstructions under the work place often interfere with the natural position of the worker, causing poor posture and discomfort. Such obstructions should not be permitted.

Arm Rest. Often the work is of such a nature that it is desirable to provide arm rests at the work place. Arm rests are most effective on work that requires little movement of the forearms, with the hands working at approximately the same position, often at some distance from the body, for long periods of time.

Foot Rest. When high chairs are used, a foot rest should be provided. The foot rest should preferably be attached to the floor or the bench, though this is less desirable, it may be fastened to the chair.

17. A chair of the type and height to permit good posture should be provided for every worker.

Good Standing Posture. When a person is standing properly, the different segments of the body-head, neck, chest, and abdomen are balanced vertically one upon the other so that her weight is borne mainly by the bony framework and a minimum of effort and strain is placed upon the muskies and ligaments. In this posture; under normal conditions the organic function respiration, circulation, digestion etc., are performed with least mechanical obstruction and with greatest efficiency.

Good Sitting Posture. The thing which should always be insisted upon in the use of the body in any way is that the body should be kept straight from the hips to the neck and should not be allowed to flex or bend at the waistline. Any position which allows this bending lowers the vitality of the individual, leads to strain of the back and naturally lessens efficiency.

The most frequent violation of the good sitting posture occurs when the individual slumps in his chair or assumes a sideways slouch, both of which are fatiguing and impair the health.

When the is seated, the chair should aid and not hinder him in maintaining good posture. A good chair should have the following features.

1. The chair should be adjustable in height so that it may be readily fitted to the particular individual who is to use it.

2. The chair should be rigidly built, preferably of steel frame with wood or padded sear and back.

3. The chair seat should be form-fitting

4. Aback rest should be provided to support the lower part of the spine.

6.4 Principles of Motion Economy as relieved of all work that can be done more advantageously by a jig, a fixture, or a foot operated device.

From observation of the tools a fixture usually found in the factory it is obvious that many tool designers do to give much thought to the principles of motion economy when they design the, in most cases the fixtures are made for hand operation only, whereas foot-operated equipment would permit the operator to have both hands free to perform other motions.

19. Two or more tools should be combined wherever possible.

It is usually quicker to turn a small two-ended tool end-for-end than it is to lay one tool down and pick up another.

20. Tools and materials should be pre-positioned whenever possible.

Pre-positioning refers to placing an object in a predetermined place in such a way that when next needed it may be grasped in the position in which it will be used. For prepositioning tools, a holder in the form of a socket, compartment, bracket, or hanger should be provided, into which or by which the tool may be returned after it is used, and where it remains in position for the next operation.

21. Where each finger performs some specific movement, such as in typewriting, the load should be distributed in accordance with the inherent capacities of the finger.

The normally right-handed person performs work with less fatigue and Greater dexterity with the right hand with left. Although most people can be trained to work equally well with either hand on most factory operations, the fingers have unequal inherent capacities for doing work. The first and second fingers of the two hands are ordinarily superior in their performance to the third and fourth fingers.

Arrangement of Typewriter Keys. A study made to determine the ideal arrangement of the keys of the typewriter for maximum efficiency also illustrates this difference in the capacities of the figures.

22. Levers, crossbars, and hand wheels should be located in such positions that the operator can manipulate them with the least change in body position and with the greatest mechanical advantage.

Some machine-tool manufactures understand that it is possible to build a machine that will perform its functions satisfactory and at the same time will be easy to operate. Unless a machine is fully automatic, the amount of work that it will produce depends to some extent upon the performance of the operator. The more convenient the machine is to operate, the greater the production is likely to be.

6.5 Summary

Principles of motion economy can be used in any office work and is divided as:

(I) Use of human body

(ii) Arrangement of work place

(iii) Design of tools and equipment

6.6 Glossary:

Momentum is the product of mass of the body and velocity.

Ballistic movement is a free-swinging

1. References:

1."Motion and Time Study-Design and measurement of work Ralph Barnes, 6th edition, John Wiley and Sons, INC (pages 221-306).

2."Introduction to Works Study", International labour office, Universal book corporation, (pages 154-170)

6.8 Self-Assessment:

1. Design the trays and list out the procedural steps to fix a nut and washer to a bolt with two hands.

2. Observe a person folding two different papers and filling them in a mailing envelop and design a new method to improve efficiency.

8. Question:

1. What is motion economy? What is its use?
2. Categorize Principles of motion economy and list them?

CHAPTER SEVEN

Ergonomics Mechanisation and Automation

The objective of this chapter is to know various arrangements to be used for maintaining health of the workers and to understand the concept of automation.

CONTENTS

7.1 Introduction

The effects of health and safety on productivity cannot be properly discussed without touching on the concept of ergonomics. This term covers a field which in recent years has expanded to an extraordinary degree and whose boundaries are far from clear. Ergonomic measures may, however, be defined as those that go beyond the mere protection of the worker's physical integrity and aim at ensuring his well-being through the attainment of optimal working conditions and by the most suitable use of his physical characteristics and physiological and psychological capabilities. Productivity is therefore not the primary objective of ergonomics but is usually one of the end products. The task is to develop the most comfortable conditions for the workers as regards lighting, climate and noise level, to reduce the physical work load (in particular in hot environments), to improve working postures and reduce the effort of certain movements, to facilities psycho-sensorial function in reading instrument displays, to make the handling of machine levers and controls easier, to make better use of spontaneous and stereotyped reflexes, to avoid unnecessary information recall efforts and so on.

Many ergonomic measures are of a kind that should be introduced at the design sage of a building, appliance or machine, or when equipment is being installed, since subsequent modifications are generally less effective and much more expensive. A machine user should incorporate the application of specific ergonomic standards in the clauses of his contract with the machine manufacture. The contract should cover safety colors, warning light and controls that have already been standardized by the International Organisation for Standardization and the International Electro technical Commission, in particular display panels and dials. In addition, attention should be given not only to item affecting productions but also to critical maintenance features.

7.2 Ergonomics (Human Engineering)

Work methods design seeks to determine the most effective combinations the man, the machine, and the working environment. In attempting to find the most effective combination, it is necessary to determine which functions can performed better by man and which by machine. Man has certain inherent ability which surpass existing machines, whereas existing machines surpass man in certain way. Also, the matter of economy enters into the determination of the man machine combination. For examples, as the volume of a manufactured product increases, greater mechanization usually becomes profitable. More and more of the activities are performed by the machine and fewer by the man. The ultimate is, of course a completely automatic process with no direct labour required.

Although engineers, physiologists, and psychologists have for many years conducted experiments dealing with work design problems, a rather highly specialized group of these people were called upon during world war-II to aid in solving man machine problems as they per trained to the design, operation and maintenance of military equipment. For example, the controls on planes, ships, and submarines became so complex that many failures resulted because the operators could not do all the things expected of them. The term human engineering was to refer to this area of activity. Human engineering reported to have as its goal "the adaptation of human tasks and working environment to the sensory, perceptual, mental, physical and other attributes of people. This adaptation for human use applied to such functions as the design of equipment, instruments, man-machine systems and consumer products, and to the development of optimum work methods and work environment".

A person ordinarily does three things in performing any task.

1. Receives information-through the sense organs, eye, ears, touch, etc.,

2. Makes decisions-acts on the information obtained and on the basis of his own knowledge.

3. Takes action-action resulting from the decision that has been made. The action may be purely physical, such as operating a machine, or it may involve communication, such as giving oral or written instructions.

The designer of machines, equipment, the work method, and the work environment must have an understanding of the wee the human being functions, his body dimensions, his physical limitations, and the conditions under which he performs most effectively. In designing any process or operation, the question arises as to just which activities should be performed by the man and which by the machine. The following summary may be useful in this connection.

Human beings appear to surpass existing machines in their ability to:

1. Detect small amounts of light or sound.

2. Receive and organize patterns of light or sound.

3. Improvise and use flexible procedures.

4. Store large amounts of information for long periods and recall relevant facts at the appropriate time.

5. Exercise Judgment.

6. Reason inductively.

7. Develop concepts and create methods.

Existing machines appear to surpass human beings in their ability to:

1. Respond quickly to control singles.

2. Apply great force smoothly and precisely

3. Perform repetitive routine tasks.

4. Store information briefly and then erase it completely

5. Perform rapid computations

6. Perform many different functions simultaneously.

7.2.1 Occupational Safety and Health Organisation

The most effective method of obtaining good results in accident prevention to establish good safety organisation within the enterprise. The organisation structure need not be formalized, nor need it require the employment or specialists its essential features should be a precise delegation of responsibilities. With structure which can ensure sustained action and a joint by employers and worker to "raise the quality of the working environment, in all its technical". This implementation the introduction of an effective occupational safety and health education are training program and the provision of the necessary first-aid and media services.

7.2.2 Safety Criteria

Studies of occupational hazards in modern industry have revealed the extremely complex nature of the possible causes of occupational accidents or diseases.

The causes of occupational accidents are never simple, even in an apparently common place accident; consequently, the number and variety of accident classifications are great. Statistics show that the most common causes of accidents are not the most dangerous machines (circular saws, spindle molding machines, power presses, for examples) nor the most dangerous substances (explosives or volatile flammable liquids), but rather quite ordinary actions like stumbling, falling the faulty handling of goods or use of hand tools, or being struck by a falling subject. Similarly, those who have accidents most frequently are not the disabled but, on the contrary, those who are the best equipped from the physical and psycho-senso-real point of view, i.e., young workers.

Technical progress has created new health hazards whilst at the same time greatly reducing the severity of conventional hazards and significantly improving the standards of machinery guarding (nevertheless, accidents do still happen even on the most carefully guarded machines). In addition, since in many countries communing accidents have now been brought under the heading of occupational accidents, the demarcation line between occupational and non-occupational hazards has become less distinct and the role of the human factor and the importance of the circumstances attempting an accident have become increasingly clear. An accident is often the result of technical, physiological and psychological factors; it depends on both machines, the environment (lighting, nose, vibration, vaporizing substances, oxygen deficiency), posture and work induced fatigue; but it is also conditioned by commuting circumstances and other activities outside the plant, specific physical or mental states. The first precaution to take in order to avoid accidents is the elimination of potential causes, both technical humans, like observance of technical rules and standards, careful supervision and maintenance, safety training for all workers add the establishment of good working relationship.

The situation relating to the causes of occupational diseases and ways of preventing them is equally complex. Technical progress has been so rapid that it has often created new and totally unrecognized hazards which have resulted in occupational diseases even before the disease was recognized as such. Yet this same technical progress has provided extremely effective tools for the early detention of signs or symptoms of occupationally induced morbidity, and even espouse tests for evaluating aa hazard before it has any obi logical effect. The study and monitoring of the working environment have, in this way, assumed a fundamental importance in the prevention of occupational diseases.

7.2.3 Fire Prevention and Protection

The first principle of prevention is to design and construct buildings with adequate fire resistance in relation to the hazards that are encountered. The second principle is to give adequate training to the workers and enforce fire prevention regulations such as bans on smoking and prohibition of the use of sources of ignition in high-risks areas. Where there is a significant fire hazard, fire protection will entail:

1. A trained fire-fighting team which carries out regular fire-fighting exercises.

2. A system of periodic inspection which may include full-time inspectors.

3. Suitable liaison with the fire bridge.

4. In large enterprises and with due regard to the costs involved, periodic, fire alarm and evaluation exercises.

7.2.4 Working Premises

As far as the layout of the work place is concerned, emphasis should be placed on the principle of isolating any operation which is hazardous or constitutes a nuisance. Walls and ceilings should have a finish which prevents the accumulation of dirt, avoids moisture absorption and, where necessary reduces noise transmission; floor coverings should be of the non-slip, non-dust-forming and easy to clean type and should, where necessary, have good electrical and thermal insulation properties.

Traffic aisles should be sufficiently wide to allow, if necessary, the simultaneous movements of vehicles and workers at peak hours (meal times, closing times), and rapid evacuation in the event of an emergency.

7.2.5 Cleanliness and Good Housekeeping

Building work premises in accordance with safety and hygiene regulations is not enough, however, if the plant or workshop is not kept clean and tidy. Good housekeeping, which when used with reference of a factory or workplace is a general term embracing tidiness and general state of repair, not only contributes to accidents prevention but also is a factor in productivity. If aisles and gangways are allowed to become cluttered with stacks of materials and other obstruction, time will be lost by workers having to clear their way for the transport of raw materials or finished products; it may take hours to find a batch of semi-finished products lost in the general disorder.

Residues Which may be source of dangerous emission of vapor, gases or dust (such as toxic liquids, refractors, asbestos and lead oxide) should be collected in a suitable way: Dust should be removed by vacuum cleaners or wet methods and chemicals should be neutralized or diluted. Deposits of certain toxic substance can be more readily identified if the floor, walls, and where necessary, the work benches are painted in a color which contrasts with that of the substance in question.

Working clothes must be kept clean in order to reduce the skin-absorption hazard of certain toxic substance (aniline and it is derivatives, benzene, its homologues and derivatives, Organ – phosphorus compounds. Tetraethyl zed and chronic or acute irritation. Prolonged contact of the skin with certain substances (especially minerals oils and aromatic hydrocarbons) may produce chronic dermatitis, sometimes followed by the development of cancer. Workers exposed to toxic substances should have twin-compartment clothing lockers to keep their working cloths separate from their other clothes so as to prevent the danger of their family being exposed to the industrial toxic substance. Similarly, it is advised to provide a centralized laundry service for working clothes in plants using highly toxic substances.

Workers employed on dirty jobs or exposed to dangerous or toxic substances should have wash-rooms with a tap for every three or four workers and a shower for every three workers (and never less than one for every eight workers) to ensure that workers do not give up taking a shower because they have to wait too long.

An important factor for the worker's health is the provision of sufficient and, where possible, cooled drinking water in the factory. This water should be approved by the health authority and its purity should be tested periodically. Where possible, the water should be on tap.

7.2.6 Lighting

It is estimated that 80 percent of the information require in doing a job is perceived visually. Good visibility of the equipment, the product and the data involved in the work process is an essential factor in accelerating production, reducing the number of defective products, reducing waste and preventing visual fatigue and headaches amongst the workers. It may also be added that both inadequate visibility and glare are frequently a cause of accidents.

Visibility depends on a number of factors: the size of the work places its distance from the eyes, the persistence of the image, the lighting intensity, the color of the work place and contrasts of color and lighting levels with the background. All these factors should study in the case of precision work, work in a dangerous environment or where there are other reasons for dissatisfaction or complaint. Lighting is often the most important factor and the one which is most easy to correct.

Natural lighting should be used wherever possible, through windows which should have an area equal to at least one-sixth of the floor area. However, since the intensity of natural lighting is extremely visible (even where the inflow can be modified by the use of shutters, blinds or shades), since its level falls rapidly as the distance from the windows increases, and since it is likely that reflected sunlight distance from the windows increases, and since it is likely that reflected sunlight will cause glare, artificial lighting must be provided to ensure suitable conditions of visibility in all seasons, at all times and in all whether conditions. Fluorescent lighting offers considerable potential for rational use, provided that glare is avoided.

7.2.7 Noise and Vibration

Code of practice on occupational safety and occupational health protection against noise and vibration in the work environment - covers responsibility of government, employers and workers, measurement, exposure limits, identification and control of hazards, protective equipment, medical examination of employees, and monitoring.

Monograph comprising a code of practice on the control of noise and vibration in the work environment - covers measurement, protective equipment and reduction of exposure time, health supervision (incl. medical examination), monitoring, etc.

This code of practice was adopted by a meeting of experts convened by the ILO (Turin 2-10 Dec. 1974. Intended to provide guidance for governments, employers and workers, it sets out the principles that should be followed for the control of workplace noise and vibration, and contains the information required for the establishment of control programs for individual plants. Definitions are followed by chapters devoted to: general principles (duties of employers and workers, co-operation, factory inspection); organizing principles of prevention; noise measurement and assessment (hearing conservation, oral communications, fatigue, measuring instruments, instrument accuracy and calibration, recording of data); noise limit levels (hearing impairment, ultrasound and infrasound, fatigue and comfort, etc.); vibration measurement; vibration limits; whole-body vibration; identification of risk areas; noise and vibration control: new equipment; noise and vibration control in the working environment; protective equipment and reduction of exposure time; health supervision. Appendices: international standards; information on health hazards of noise, ultrasound, infrasound and vibration; maximum allowable levels of ultrasound; noise hazard contours; signs indicating noise zones, etc.

7.2.8 Arrangements of working time

Since they tend to reduce amount of peak-hour road and rail traffic and allow workers to shop and to make use of public services during the week, without requesting special permission from their employer. A major innovation in the arrangement of working time was carried through when variable of flexible patterns of work were successfully adopted in certain European countries.

Shift work is common is several industries, particularly for certain operations such as oil refining, continuous steel production, and so on. Shift work may take one of three forms:

(a) Two shifts of eight hours each (indicated as 2 X 8) with an interruption of work at the end of the day and of the week;

(b) Three shifts or eight hours each (or 3 X 8) with an interruption for the week-end; or

(c) Fully continuous operations with no stoppages and including work on Sunday, and public holidays. Such a system needs more than three shifts (4 X 8 or 5 X 8).

7.3 Mechanization and Automation:

Over the centuries, man has been finding easier and better ways to produce the goods and services he needs and wants. Work originally consists of activities performed with the bare hands; then simple tools were devised, and later power-driven machines. Now fully automatic equipment makes it possible to remove much of the burden of manual work from the man and transfer it to the machine. We have long recognized that an increases in productivity per man-hour was a major factor in bringing about improvement in our standard of living. Few people advocate using human labour to do work that can be done better and cheaper by machines. The day is far distant, however, when manual work in industry will disappear some activities are too complex to be mechanized and must therefore be performed manually. Some tasks occur so seldom that it not economical to use machines. Moreover, others factors may affect the extent to which mechanization should be used in a given situation – factors such as quality, yield, material utilization, safety, availability of qualified workers, availability of chapter, the probable life of the produce being made.

Since the application of principles of motion economy ordinarily call for a very small capital investment and a minimum of design cost, it is suggested that the best manual method or the best combination or manual and machine methods be developed and use as a basis for evaluating a proposed mechanized or automated process. For example, one company makes it a practice to determine and evaluate alternative methods. If a large volume fairly complex operation is to be considered, a comparison would be made of the estimated cost to do each element or each sub operation manually and also automatically. For example, in a punch-press operation the parts could be manually or automatically fed, the press could be actuated manually or automatically, and the finished parts could be removed by hand or rejected automatically. The cost to install and maintain each of the automatic components would have to be evaluated against the costs of the manual method. However, an efficient manual method should be used as the basic for compassion.

7.4 Summary

Human engineering considers the relationship between the physical and mental characteristics (capacities and limitations) of people and the jobs they do and or the machines they operate. It is used in the design of many products, machines and working environments. In offices, noise reducing baffles, properly designed desks, chairs, office equipment and soft background music are result of Human engineering consideration.

7.5 Glossary

ERGONOMICS may be defined as the measure that go beyond the mere protection of the workers physical integrity and aim ensuring his wellbeing.

7.6 References

"MOTION AND TIME STUDY – Design and measurement of work" Ralf. M. Barnes, sixth edition, John-Wiley & sons, Inc. (pages209-211).

CHAPTER EIGHT

QUALITY CONTROL – 1

The objective of this and text chapter is to reader understand the basics of Quality.

CONTENTS

8.1 Introduction

When the expression "quality product" is used, we usually think in terms of a good or excellent product. In industry, a quality product is one that fulfills customer's expectations. Control is the process of regulating or directing an activity to verify its conformance to a standard and to take corrective action if required. Therefore, quality control is the regulatory process for those activities which measure a products performance, compare that performance with established standards, and pursue corrective action regardless of where those activities occur.

Statistical quality control is a branch of quality control. It is the collection, analysis, and interpretation of data to solve a particular problem. In order to attain and maintain a quality product, a number of different techniques are needed. As quality has become more important, an independent audit or evaluation of the quality function is needed by top management. Quality has become more important; an independent audit or evaluation of the quality function is needed by top management. Quality assurance is that activity which evaluates the quality function. It can be compared to the independent audit of the finance function;

The objective of quality control is to provide the customer with the best product at a minimum cost. This objective is accomplished by improvements in the product design, consistency in the manufacture of the product, reduction in manufacturing costs, and improved employee morale.

CUSTOMER

PRODUCT SERVICE MARKETING

Ensure Quality Determines Customer
Of performance Quality Requirements
PACKAGING AND SHIPPING QUALITY CONTROL PRODUCT ENGINEERING
Preserve and Protects Translates Requirements
Quality of the Product into Quality oriented Designs
INSPECTION AND TEST PURCHASING
Appraising Quality Procures Quality
of Conformance Materials and Components
MANUFACTURING MANNUFACTURING ENGINEERING
Transforms Designs and Develops Quality
Material into Oriented Processes and
Quality Products Procedures
Department responsible for quality

A quality assurance system is an effective method of attaining and maintaining the desired quality standards. It is based on the fact that quality is the responsibility of all functions. Evaluations are usually conducted each year to determine which elements and subsystems need improvement. The overall rating provides a comparison with past performance or with other plants of a multi plant corporation.

8.2 Fundamentals of Statistics:

The word statistics has two generally acceptance meanings

1. A collection of quantitative data pertaining to any subject or group, especially when the data are systematically gathered and collated. Examples of this meaning are blood pressure statistics, to name football game, employment statistics, and accident statistics, to name a few.

2. The science that deals with the collection, tabulation, analysis interpretation and presentation of quantitative data.

There are two phases of statistic.

1. Descriptive or deductive, statistics, with endeavors to describe and analyze subject or group.

2. Inductive statistics, which endeavors or determine from a limited amount of data (sample) an important conclusion about a much large amount of data (universe). Since these conclusion or inferences cannot be started with absolute certainty, the language of probability is often used.

Variable are those quality characteristics which are measurable, such as a weight measured in grams. Attributes, on the other hand, are those quality characteristics which are classified as either conform or not conforming to specifications. In other words, attributes are either good or bad, while variables indicate the degree of "goodness" or "badness".

A variable that is capable of any degree of subdivisions referred to as continuous. Variables that exhibit gaps are called discrete. While many quality characteristics are stated as at tributes. Frequently, those characteristics which are judged by visual observation are classified as attributes.

8.2.1 Measures of Central Tendency

A measure of central tendency of a distribution is a numerical value that describes the central position of the data or how the data tend to build up in the center. There are three techniques in common use (1) the arithmetic mean, (2) the median, and (3) the mode.

Mean:

The arithmetic mean, more simply the mean, is the sum of the values in a distribution divided by the number if values. It is the most common measures of central tendency.

Median:

Another measure of central tendency is the median, which is defined as the value which divides a series of ordered observation so that the number of items above it is equal to the number below it.

Mode:

The mode (Mo) of a number is that value which occurs with the greatest frequency. It is possible for the mode to be nonexistent in a series of numbers or to have more than one value.

The mean is the most commonly used measured of central tendency. It is used when the distribution is symmetrical or not appreciable skewed to the right or left; when additional statistics, such as measures of dispersion, control charts, and so on, are to be computed based on the mean, and when a stable value is needed or inductive statistics.

8.2.2 Measures of Dispersion:

It describes how the data are spread out or scattered on each side the central value.

Range:

The range of series of numbers is the difference between the largest and smallest values or observations.

Standard Deviation:

The standard deviation is measure of the dispersion, and is the one most commonly used. It is the root-men-square deviation of the observation values about their mean and is some-times referred to as the RMS deviation.

Mean Decimation:

The mean deviation (MD) is the average deviation of a series of numbers from their mean. In averaging the deviations, no account is taken of signs, and all deviations, whether plus or minus, are treated as positive. The mean deviation is also called the mean absolute deviation (MAD) or average deviation (AD).

Quartile Deviation:

The median divides the distribution in half and the quartile divides the distribution into quarters. There are three quartiles in a distribution. The first quartile of a distribution is that value which has 25% of the values below it, and the third quartile has 75% of the values below it.

8.2.3 Concept of a Universe and a Sample:

At this point in the chapter, it is desirable to examine the concept of a universe and sample. In order to construct a frequency distribution of the weights of steel shafts, a small portion, or sample, is selected to represent all the steel shafts. Similarly, the data collected concerning the passenger car speeds represented only a small portion of all the passenger cars. The universe is the whole collection of measurements, and in the examples above, the universe would be all the steel shafts and all the passenger cars. When means, standard deviations, and other measures are computed for samples, they are referred to as statistics, since the composition of samples will fluctuate, the computed statistics will be larger or smaller than their true universe values, or parameters. Parameters are considered to be fixed reference (standard) values or parameters. Parameters are considered to be fixed reference (standard) values or the best estimate of these value which is available at a particular time.

8.3. Control Charts for Variables;

8.3.1 Variation

One of the axioms or truisms of manufacturing is that no two objects are ever made exactly alike. In fact, the variation concept is a law of nature. In that no two natural items in any category are the same. The variation may be quite large and easily noticeable, such as the height of humans, ire the variation may be very small, such as the weight of fiber-tipped pens. The ability to measure this variation in the product is necessary before I can be controlled.

There are categories of vibration in the part

1. With-in Variation. This type of variation is illustrated by the surface roughness of a piece where in one portion of the surface rougher than another portion, or the width of one end of a keyway varies from the other end.

2. Piece to Piece variation. This type of variation occurs among piece produced at the same time. Thus, the light intensity of four consecutive light bulbs produced from a machine will be different.

3. Time-to-Time variation. This type of variation is illustrated by the difference in product produced at different time of the data. The product produced in the early morning would be different from that produced later in the day or as a cutting toll wear, the cutting characteristics change.

There are four factors that contribute to these variations, and they are processes, materials, operators and miscellaneous. The first source of variation is the process. This source includes tool wear, machine vibration work holding-device positioning, and hydraulic and electrical fluctuations.

The second source of variation is the material. Since variation occurs in the finished products, it must also occur in the raw material (which was someone else finished product). A third and possibly the greatest source of variation is the operator. This source of variation includes the method by which the operator performs the operation.

The fourth source of variation is miscellaneous. This source includes environmental factors, such as heat, light, radiation and humidity. For example, when the outside humidity is high, the moisture content of paper stock changes and adversely affects the process. Included in this category is the inspection process. Thus, faculty inspection equipment, ire the incorrect application of a quality standard, or too heavy a pressure on a micrometer, can be cause of the incorrect reporting of variation.

As long as these four sources of variation (process, materials, operators and miscellaneous) fluctuate in a normal or excepted manner, a stable pattern of many chances cause of variation develops. Chance causes of variation are inevitable and because they are very small in magnitude and therefore readily identified, are classified as assignable cause. When only chance causes are present in a process, the process is considered to be in control. However, when an assignable cause of variation is also present, the variation will be excessive and the process is classified as out of control or beyond the expected normal variation.

8.3.2 Purpose of Control charts:

1. To provide information for current decisions in regard to recently produced items. Thus, the control chart issued as one source of information to help decide whether an item to items should be released to the customers or some alternative disposition made, such as sorting and repairing.

2. To provide information for current decisions in regard to the production process. Thus, the control chart is used to decide when a normal pattern of variation occurs and the process should be left alone, and when an unstable pattern of variation is occurring, which requires action to find and eliminate the disturbing or assignable causes.

3. To provide information for decisions in regard to produced specifications. Production processes, or inspection procedures. Thus, data from the control charts can be used to establish the product specifications, or to evaluate the production process, or to change the inspection procedures.

4. To provide a method of instruction operating and supervisory personnel in the techniques of quality control.

8.3.3 Control Chart Techniques:

In order to establish a pair of control charts for the average and the range ®, it is

desirable to follow a set procedure. The steps in this procedure are as follows:

1. Select the quality characteristic

2. Choose the rational subgroup

3. Collect the data

4. Determine the trial control limits

5. Establish the revised control limits

8.3.4 Various Control Charts:

X – Chart R - Chart

$UCLX = X + 3\,\sigma$ $X\ UCLR = R + 3\,\sigma\ R$

$LCLX = X - 3\,\sigma$ $X\ LCLR = R - 3\,\sigma\ R$

Where UCL = Upper Control Limit

LCL = Lower Control Limit

$\sigma\ X$ = Standard deviation of the subgroup means (X's)

$\sigma\ R$ = Standard deviation of the range

σ - Chart

$UCL = \sigma$

$LCL = \sigma$

σ = average of the subgroup standard deviations B3, B4 = factors for obtaining of the control limits for X and σ charts.

The natural pattern of variations has (1) about two-thirds of the points near the center solid line or central value, (2) a few points closed to the control limits, (3) points located back and forth across the center line, (4) point balanced on both sides of the center line or central value, and (5) no point beyond the control limits.

8.3.5 Process in Control:

Control limits are usually established at three standard deviations from the central value. They are as a basic dot judge whether there is evidence of lack of control. The choice of 3 limits is an economic one with respect to two types of errors that can occur. One error, called Type 1 by statisticians, occurs when looking for an assignable cause of variation when in really a chance cause is present. The other type error, called Type II, occurs when assuming that a chance cause of variation is present when in reality there is an assignable cause.

When a process in control, only chance causes of variation are present. Small variations in machine performance, operator performance and material characteristics are expected and are considered to be part of a stable process.

When a process is in control, certain particular advantages accrue to the manufacturer and purchaser.

1. Individual units of the product will be more uniform or stated another way, there will be less variation among parts.

2. Since the product is more inform, fewer samples are needed to judge the quality. Therefore, the cost of inspection can be reduced to a minimum. This advantage is extremely important when100% conformance to specifications is too essential.

3. The process capability or spread of the process is easily attained from 6 or by multiplying the square root of the sample size by the difference between the control limits. With a knowledge of the process capability, a number of reliable decisions relative to specifications can be made, such as;

a) To decide the product specifications

b) To decide the amount of rework or scrap when there is insufficient tolerance.

c) To decide whether to produce the product to tight specifications and permit interchangeability of components or to produce the product to lose specifications and use selective matching of components.

4. The percentage of product that falls within any pair of values may be predicted with the highest degree of assurance. For examples, this advantage can be very important when adjusting machines to obtain different percentage of items below, or above particular values.

8.3.6 Process Spread and Specifications:

While specifications can be established by the product engineer without regard for the spread of the process, serious situation can result when this type of action is adopted. There are three situations; (1) When the process spread is less than the difference between specifications, (2) when the process spread is equal to the difference between specifications, (3) and when the process spread is greater than difference between specifications.

Case : 6σ LU-L. This situation, where the spread of the process (6σ) is less than difference between specifications. (U-L) , is the most desirable case. Figure illustrates this ideal relationship by the distribution of individual values labeled A. since the Specifications are appreciably greater than the process spread, no difficulty in encountered even when there is a substantial shift in the process, average, as shown by the distribution at B. at C shift in the dispersion is illustrated, and all the individual values are between specifications.

Case is economically advantageous since an out-of-control condition, as illustrated at B and C does not produce defective product. Therefore, frequent machine adjustments or searches for assignable causes are not necessary. In fact, this satisfactory state of affairs suggests that the control chart may be discontinued.

Case II: 6σ = UK. Figure 2 illustrates this cause where the spreads of the process, or process capability, is equal to the difference between specifications. The frequency distribution at A presents a natural pattern of variation. However, when there us a shift in the process average, as indicated at B, or c change in the dispersion, as indicated at C, the individual values exceed the specifications. As long as the process remains in control as indicated at A, no defective product is produced; however, when the process to put is control as indicated at B and C, defective product is being produced. Therefore, assignable causes of variation must be corrected as soon as they occur.

Case III : 6σ = U-L. When the spread of the process of process capability is greater than the difference between specifications, an undesirable situation exists. Figure 3 illustrates this case. Even though a natural paternal pattern of variation is occurring, as shown by the frequency distribution at A, some of the individual values are greater than the upper specification and are less than the lower specification. This case presents the unique situation where the process is in control, but effective product is produced. In other where the process is control , be defective product is produced. In other words, the process is not capable of manufacturing a product that will meet the specification.

8.4 Summary:

Quality is not the responsibility of any one person or department: it is every one's job. The responsibility for quality so delegated to the various departments with the authority to make decisions. In addition, a method of accountability, such as cost or number defective is included with that responsibility and account ability. Quality control is to be carried out at all necessary stages of production.

8.5 Glossary

QUALITY product is one that fulfills customer's expectations.

Quality control is the regulatory process for those activities which measure a product's performance, compare that performance with established standard, and purse corrective action regardless of where those activities occur.

Quality assurance is that which evaluates the quality function. It can be compared to the independent audit of the finance function.

8.6 Reference

"Quality control – a practical approach" Dale H. Esterified, Prentice Hall; INC., (Pages 1-94).

8.7 Questions for Discussion

1. Imagine you are producer of (a) leather shoes, (b) castings and list out various quality control points during different stage of production

2. List out attributes and variables for a product.

8.8 Questions

1. What are the departments responsible for quality control?

2. What are the purposes of QC charts?

Quality Control – 2

CONTENTS

9.1 Control charts for Attributes:

The term attributes, as used in quality, refer to those quality characteristics which are either good or bad; they conform Specifications or they do not confirm to specifications.

There are two types of attributes.

1. Where measurements are not possible, for example visually inspected items such as color, missing parts, scratches, and damage.

2. Where measurements can be made but are not made because of time, cost, or need. In order words, while the diameter of a hold can be measured with an inside micrometer, it may be more convenient to use 'go no go' gage and determine if the part is good or bad.

Some confusion occurs between the term's "defects" and "defective". A defect is quality characteristics that does not conform to specifications. On the other hand, a defective part is a part that is not usable because it had one or more defects. A defective can have many defects.

Control Charts for Faction Defective:

P – Chart

The P chart is used for data that consist of the ratio of the number of occurrences of an event to the total number of occurrences, it is used in quality control to report the fraction defective in a product, quality characteristics, or group of quality characteristics. As such, the fraction defective is the ratio of the number effective in a sample or sub group to the fraction defective is the ratio of the number effective din a sample or subgroup to the total number in the sample or sub group. In symbolic terms the formula is

$P = npn$

Where p = fraction defective of the sub group or sample

n = number in the sample of subgroup

np = number defective

control Chart for number of Defects

the other type of attribute chart is a number-of-defects chart, which is referred to a c-chart. By definition, c is equal to the number of defects. While a p chart controls the fraction defective in the product, the c-chart controls the number of defects in the product. An item is classifying as defective when it has one or many defects.

9.2 Lot-by-Lot Acceptance Sampling by Attributes

9.2.1 Fundamental Concepts

Lot-of-Lot acceptance sampling by attributes is the most common type of sampling. With this type of sampling, a predetermined number of units (sample) from each lot is inspected by attributed by attributes. It the amount defective is less than the prescribed minimum, the lot is accepted, if not, the lot is rejected as being below standard. Each lot in the shipment or order is sampled and either rejected or accepted. Acceptance sampling can be used either for the amount defective or for defects per unit. To Simplify the presentation in this chapter, the amount defective is used; however, it is understood that the information is also applicable to defect per unit. Sampling plans are established for each class of defect severity (critical, major, minor) or on a demerit per-unit basis.

Acceptances sampling of the product is most likely to be used in one of these situations.

1. When the test is destructive (such as a test on an electrical fuse or a tensile test), sampling is necessary: otherwise, all the product will be destroyed by testing.

2. When the cost of 100% inspection is high, sampling can save money.

3. When there are many similar items to be inspected, sampling will produce as good, if not better results than 100% inspection. This is true because, with manual inspection, fatigue and bore born cause a higher percentage of defective material to be passed than would occur in a sampling plan.

Advantages and Disadvantages of sampling

When sampling is compared with 100% inspection; it has the following

advantages:

1. More economical, owing to fewer inspections

2. Less handling damage during inspection

3. Fewer inspectors, thereby simplifying recruiting, training, and supervising.

4. Upgrading the inspection job from monotonous piece=by=piece decisions to lot-by-lot decisions

5. Applicable to destructive testing.

6. Rejection of entire lots rather than the return of defectives, thereby providing stronger motivation for improvement.

Inherent disadvantages of acceptance sampling are:

1. There are certain risks of accepting "bad" lots and of rejecting "good" lots.

2. More time and effort are devoted to planning and documentation. Less information is usually provided about the product.

Types of Sampling Plans:

There are three types of sampling plans: single, double and multiple. In the single sampling plan, one sample is taken from the lot and a decision sample. This type of sampling plan was described earlier in the chapter.

Double sampling plans are somewhat more complicated. On the initial sample decision, based on the inspection results is made whether (1) to accept the lot, (2) to reject the lot, or (3) to take another sample. If a second sample is required, the results of the inspection and first inspection are used to reject or accept the lot.

9.2.2 OC Curve:

An excellent evaluation technique is an operating characteristic (OC) curve. In judging a particular sampling plan, it is desirable to know the probability that a lot submitted with a certain percent defective, 100p', will be accepted or rejected. The OC Curve will provide this information, and a typical OC Curve is shown below.

OC Curve Properties:

Acceptance sampling plans with similar properties can give different OC Curves. Four of these properties and the OC Curve information are given in the information that follows.

1. Sampling size as a Fixed Percentage of lot Size. Prior the use of statistical concepts for acceptance sampling, inspectors were usually instructed to sample a fixed percentage of the lot. If this value is, say, 10% of the

N = 900 n = 90 C = 0

N = 300 n = 30 C = 0

N = 90 n = 9 C = 0

Figure 2 Shows the OC Curves for the three plans, and it is evident that they offer different levels of protection. For example, lots from a process that is 5% defective will be accepted 2% of the time for lot sizes of 900, 22% of the time for lot sizes of 300, and 63% of the time for lot sizes of 90.

Type A OC curves give the probability of accepting an isolated finite lot. With a finite situation of the hyper geometric is used to calculated to acceptance probabilities. As the lot size of a type A curve increase, it approaches the type B curve and will become almost identical when the lot size is at least 10 times the sample size (N 0.10). In comparing the type, A and type B curves the type A curve is always lower than the type B curve.

2. Fixed Sample size. When a fixed or constant sample size is used, the OC curves are very similar. Figure 3 illustrates this property for the type A situation where n is 10% of N. naturally, for type B curves or when n 10% of N, the curves are identical. The sample size has more to do with the sample shape of the OC curve and the resulting quality protection than does the lot size.

3. As sample Size Increases, the Curve Becomes Steeper. Figure 4 illustrates the Change in the Shape of the OC curve. As the sample size increases, the slope of the curve becomes steeper and approaches a straight vertical line. Sampling plans with large sample sizes are better able to discriminate between good and bad quality lots. Therefore, the consumer has fewer lots bad quality acceptance and the producer fewer lots of good quality rejected.

4. As the acceptance Number Decreases, the Curve Becomes Steeper. The change in the shape of h OC curve as the acceptance number changes is shown in figure 5. As the acceptance number decreases the curve becomes steeper. This fact has frequently been incorrectly used to justify the use of sampling plans with acceptance number of zero. However, the OC curve for N = 2000, n = 300, C = 2, which is shown by the dashed line, is steeper than the plan with C = 0. Sampling plans with acceptance numbers greater than zero can actually be superior to those with zero. In addition, many producers and consumers have psychological aversion to lanes that reject lots when only one defective is found in the sample. Therefore, sampling plans with higher samples sizes and acceptance numbers are usually considered to be better.

9.2.3 Consumer Producer Relationship:

When acceptance sampling is used, there is a conflicting interest between the consumer and the producer. The producer wants all goods lots accepted and the consumer wants all bad lots rejected. Only an ideal sampling plan which has an OC curve that is a vertical line can satisfy both the producer and consumer.

The producer's risk, which is represented by the symbol alfa, is the probability of rejection of a "good" lot.

Associated with the producer's risk is numerical definition of "bad" quality, called lot to relance present defective (LTPD): The LTPD is the percent defective in the lot which can be tolerated by the consumer.

He averages outstanding quality is the (AOQ) is another technique for the evaluation of a sampling plan. The average outgoing quality is the quality that leaves the inspection operation. It is assumed that any rejected lots have been rectified or sorted and returned with 100% good product.

9.3 Acceptance Sampling Plans for Variables

While attribute sampling plans are the most common type of acceptance sampling, there are situations where variable sampling is required. Variable sampling plans are based on the sample statistics of men and/or standard deviation and the type of frequency distribution. Advantage and Disadvantage. Variable sampling has the principal advantage that the sample size is considerably less than with attribute sampling. In addition, Variable sampling provides a better basis for improving quality and gives more information for decision making.

One of the disadvantages of variable sampling is that only one characteristic can be evaluated; a separate plan is required for each quality characteristic. Variable sampling usually involves higher administrative, clerical, and equipment costs. Furthermore, the distribution of the universe has to be known or estimated.

Variable sampling is commonly applied to in house inspection, where the distribution is known and where the inspection is costly, such as destructive testing.

9.4 Reliability

Simply stated, reliability is quality over the long run. Quality is the condition of the product during manufacturing or immediately afterward, whereas reliability is the ability of the product to perfume its intended function over a period of time. A product that "works" for a long period of time is a reliable one. Since all units of product will fails at different times, reliability is a probability.

A more precise definition is: Reliability is the probability that a product will perform its intended function satisfactorily for a prescribed life under certain stated environmental conditions. From the definition, there are four factors associated with reliability: (1) numerical value, (2) intended function (3) life, and (4) environmental conditions.

The numerical value is the probability that failure of the product will not occur during a particular time. Thus, value of 0.93 would represent that probability that 93 of 100 products would function after a prescribed period of time and 7 products would fail before the prescribed period of time. Particular probability distributions can be used to describe the failure of units of product.

The second factor concerns the intended function of the product. Products are designed for particular applications and are expected to be able to perform those applications. For example, an electric hoist is expected to life a certain design load; it is not expected to lift a load that exceeds the design specification.

The third factor in the definition its reliability is the intended life of the product; in other words, how long the product is expected to last. Thus, the life of automobile tries is specified by different values. Such as 36 months or 48,000 Km. Depending on the construction of the tire. Product life is specified as a function of usage, time, or both.

The last factor in the definition, involves the environmental conditional conditions. A product that is designed to function indoors; such as n upholstered chair cannot be expected to function reliably outdoor in the sun, wind and precipitation. The area of environmental conditions also includes the storage and then the environmental conditional while the product is in use.

System Reliability:

As products become more complex (have more components), the chance of failure increases. The method of arranging the components affects the reliability of the entire system. Components can be arranged in series, parallel or a combination. Figure 6 illustrates the various arrangements.

When components are arrangement are arranged in series, the reliability of the system is the product of the individual components. Thus, for the series arrangement of Figure 6a, the series reliability Rs, is calculated as follows:

Rs = (RA)(RB)(RC)

= (0.95)(0.75)(0.99)

= 0.71

As component are added to the series, the system reliability decreases.

When components are arranged in series in series, the failure of any component causes failure of the system. This is not because when the components are arranged in parallel. When a component fails, the product continues to function using another component until all parallel components have failed. Thus, for the parallel arrangement in figure 6b the parallel reliability, Rp. Is calculated as

Follows:

RP = 1 - (1 – REL) (1 – RJ)

= 1 – (1 - 0.75) (1 – 0.84)

= 0.96

As the number of components in parallel increases, the reliability increases. The reliability for a parallel arrangement of component in greater than the reliability of the individual component.

Most complexed products are combination of series and parallel arrangements of components. This is illustrated in figure 6c, where in part B is replaced by the parallel components, part I and J. The reliability of the combination, RC, is calculated as follows:

(c) Combination Arrangement

Figure 6 methods of arranging components in 3 ways.

9.5 Quality Costs

Quality costs cross department lines by involving all activities of the company-purchasing, manufacturing, design, and quality control personnel salaries, are readily identical; other costs, such as those associated with scrap and rework, are more difficult to identify and allocate. There are customer-dissatisfaction costs and loss-of-reparation costs which are difficult, if not impossible, to measure.

Quality costs are a significant management tool. They provide:

1. A method of assessing the overall effectiveness of the quality program.

2. A means of establishing programs to meet overall needs.

3. A method of ermining problem areas and action priorities.

4. A technique to determine the optimum amount of effort between the various quality activities.

5. Information for pricing products or bidding on jobs.

Producing items that have a high level of quality is not enough. The consolidate achieving that quality must be carefully managed so that the long-range effect the quality costs on the company's profits is a desirable one. This is the true means of the quality effort.

9.6 Glossary

DEFECT is a quality characteristic that not conform to specifications.

DEECTIVE part contains many defects.

PRODUCER'S RISK is the probability of rejection of good lot.

CONSUMER'S RISK is the probability of accepting of a bad lot.

9.7 Reference

1."Quality control-a practical approach" Dale. B e starfield. Pritchel, Inc. (pages 117-234).

2."Operations Management" Kostas N Devastates, Mc-Graw-Hill, International Book co.,

9.8 Question for Self-Assessment

1. Discuss the pros cons of sampling with suitable examples.

9.9 Questions

1. Draw a p chart assuming data.

2. Distinguish between p & c charts.

CHAPTER TEN

The Role of OR

The Role of OR

CONTENTS

10.1 WHAT'S IT ALL ABOUT?

Life consists of continuous process of making decisions and solving problems. From the days of childhood to our teenage years and then our adult lives, we try to stay healthy, be happy, and do interesting things. In the process we make numerous types of decisions. The environment in which we live is complex with various components such as laws, regulations, morality, socio-economic realities, uncertainly about the future, many diseases, and the like. Thus, decision making is never simple.

Although we make decisions every day, we rarely spend time thinking about how we actually do make decisions. Perhaps we are too busy making decisions to think about decision making. Since we want to be successful in almost everything we do, we would like to do the right things at the right times. No one is a perfect decision maker, but each of us would like to be a successful one at least for important decision.

As individuals, we are experienced decision makers. Every day we make many routine decisions how to dress, which road to take to school, where to have lunch, and so on. We also make many important decisions whether to look for a part-time job at the library or at a local bank, whether to take computer science or anthropology as our Minot. Whether to join a karate club or a bridge club, whether to go to graduate school or look for a job, and the like. Although the consequences of some of these decisions may be relatively minor, important decisions such as choosing a spouse or career can change our lives.

Some people believe that good decision makers are boom worth special abilities. But we believe, and many empirical studies support our position, that decision making abilities can be acquired through learning and experience. Managerial decision making is not far different from personal decision making. However, the magnitude, the nature, and the possible consequence are enormously greater tor managerial problem. Thus, purpose in studying Management Science is to learn the basics of rational decision making and how they can be applied to solving teal world management problems.

A noted educator once stated that every child should know at least two foreign languages. English and Mathematics. This educator had a rare perceptiveness in his definition of mathematics as a language. Mathematics is the language of rational thought. Thus, we will use mathematics in learning to be rational, consistent and systematic in generating useful information for decision making. Mathematics allows us to be precise and succinct in expressing our thoughts. Furthermore, mathematics enables us to manipulate important characteristics of problems in answering "What if" questions, that makes mathematics a perfect tool for rational decision making.

Discussion of mathematics brings up an interesting and practical question: can we realty be perfectly rational in decision making? We know we cannot. Decision making in human organizations to never precise. We must analyze the inexact nature of human problems with imprecise tools and our limited analytical abilities. The manager knows his and therefore cannot be a total idealist. He or she must get desired results through practical means. Then, the rational decision-making process based on mathematics must be practical. It can be and has been in may real world applications.

10.2 MANAGEMEN AND DECISION MAKING

The livelihood of an organization is management. In spite of all else, if management falters, an organization cannot long survive. Although management is vital to our society, we have no universal definition of management; management has different meanings to different people. We know pretty much what a private does in the army, a secretary in an office, an assembly line worker in a General Motors plant, a sales person in a shoe store, and a nurse in a municipal hospital. However, we have no standard view of a manager's job. What a manager is and what he does depends entirely upon the organization, the geographical location, the department, the expertise of the manager, the number of people working under him, and many other related factors.

Over a half century ago, Mary Parker Follet defined management as "getting things done though people" . this broad and vague definition is meant as a dynamic living system, which integrates human. Financial and physical resources in such an effective way that the output becomes greater than the simple sequence of its inputs. Thus, management emphasizes the following factors:

1. Determination of definite directions for the organisation-a of objectives:
2. Search for efficient way to achieve the objectives through evaluating feasible alternatives;
3. Analysis of the environmental constants, both external and internal to the organization.

Traditionally, management has been regarded as the art of "getting things done: Thus emphasizes the "art" of performing the job. The individual manager's behavior leadership qualities, with a strong connotation of a military commander's abilities, is an example of the "art" we are talking about. On the other hand, many recent studies have emphasized the "science" aspect of management—analytical approaches to problem solving and decision making.

In reality, we believe management is a combination of art and science in which both the behavioral and systematic approaches are required. In science, we can predict the phenomenon with a definite probability of occurrence when the ingredients of a process are accurately determined. For example, we can foretell with 99.99 per cent accuracy the result of a chemical process when certain chemicals are added together in a given environment. However, such accuracy of scientific experimentation or prediction is impossible in a management price because the ingredients (people and other resources) are unpredictable and the environment is dynamic.

Management is a dynamic system which involve constantly changing environments, technologies and philosophies. Thus, the basic function of modern management has become management of disturbance. Problem solving, or decision making. Decision making is the most fundamental function management. As a matter of fact, Herbert A. Simon, an eminent scholar of management and a Nobel laureate in 1978, states that decision making is synonymous with management. Also, David W Miller and Martin K Stare, professors or management at Colombia University and well-known experts in management, point out that managers are evaluated on the basic of their performance in decision making.

In order to improve the quality so decision making, organizations and managers constantly seek ways to be more rational and systematic in making decisions. Thus, management science has become an integral part of modern management. Management science is a discipline which includes a host of rational approaches to management science and decision making. The central theme of management science is the application if scientific and rational making. The central theme of management science is the application if scientific and rational methodologies to the process of management.

10.3 RATIONALLY IN DECISION MAKING:

A well-known scientist decided that he had been a bachelor long enough, or at least that he should seriously consider whether to get married or not, and if so, to whom. Being a rational man, he sat down and enumerated the advantages and disadvantages of the marital state and the kind of qualities that he should look for in choosing a wife. As for the advantages, I quote from his nots: "Children (if it please God), constant companion (and friend in old age), charms of music and female chit chat". Among the disadvantages: Terrible loss of time its anomy children, forced to gain one's bread. Sighting about no society". But he continued, what is the use of working without sympathy from near and dear friends? Who are near and dear friends to the old, except relatives? And his consolation was, My God, it is intolerable to think of spending one's whole life like a bee, working, working and nothing after all. No, no, won't do Imagine living all one's day solitarily in a smokey, dirty London house. Only picture to yourself a nice soft wife no a sofa, with a good fire and books and music perhaps. Compare this yourself a nice soft wife on a sofa, with a good fire and Street. His conclusion: "Marry, marry, marry," Having decided that he ought to get married and having listed the desirable qualities of a future spouse, he then proceeded to look for a suitable candidate. He had several female cousins so there was no need to search outside the family circle. He dispassionately compared their attributes with his list of objective and constraints, made his choice and proposed to her needless to say, he lived ever after. The scientist in question: Charles Darwin ; the year1837.

The above story points out several important aspects of decision making .The first is that the rational decision-making effort is really nothing new. As a matter of fact, the primary distinguishing characteristic of mankind has been the capacity to learn about his environment and to use such knowledge in an organized effort to accomplish desired goals. Some academicians take the concept of decision-making philosopher . There is no practical value in seeing a detailed genealogy of rational decision making. It should suffice to say that rational decision-making effort has always been a major task of mankind.

The second aspect that we want to point out in the Darwin story is that decision making is constrained by environmental factors. Charles Darwin was a superb scientist. Thus, he was able to be rational in selecting his wife. The six wives of Henry VIII certainly must have wished that he Waa more rational in solving his marital problems. For some reason, Darwin Limited his search for a bride to the family circle. Although he thought he made the best decision. It might not have been the best decision. This special constraint he imposed have been due to his family training, his personality, or the accepted social norm during that period of time in England. In other words, the way we define the decision environment presents a host of constraints to fine decision-making process.

The third aspect of the Darwin story which deserves our attention is that complex real-world problems usually involve multiple, sometimes conflicting objectives. Indeed, management by multiple objectives is a fact of life in the manager's job. This particular element of complexity has been an important area of research in management science during the past ten years.

Whenever we discuss rationally in decision making, two basic approaches emerge; the scientific method and the concept of "economic person". We will now discuss them in detail.

10.4 MANAGEMENT SCIENCE AND SYSTEMS APPROACH

The scientific method has evolved over a long period of time as a set if systematic steps for conducting research in the physical sciences – physics, chemistry, biology, astronomy, geology, and so on. It has been said that Sir Francis Bacon was the first was the first person who formally suggested the method over four hundred years ago. Although the scientific method was established for the physical sciences, management scientists have borrowed the concept liberally for management decision making.

Step 1. Define the Decision Problem:

This first step is the most crucial and difficult part, suppose you defined your problem as "Should I work at the Pizza Parlor or the Radio Shack?" This statement excludes not only other workplaces but also many other types of decisions you face, such as what to do about your fast! Declining grades, how to handle the upcoming job interview, and where to spend the spring; break skiing in Colorado or hitchhiking to Florida. You may want to evaluate all of our pressing problems and come up with the most urgent one.

Suppose you decided to redefine your problem as follows: "I am broke. I need to make some money by taking a part-time job really quick." The nature of the problem has been changed drastically in that ft has opened up all the possible work opportunities – the local library, the pizza parlor, a branch bank, K Mart, McDonald's Radio Shack, Pont ills, and so on. Finding a good solution to a right problem Is far superior to getting the best solution to a wrong problem.

Step 2, search for Data and Information:

In order to understand fully the nature of the problem at hand and its relationship to other problems, it is essential to have relevant problems. The problem discussed above may be due not to your lack of funds but to your undisciplined, too frequent social activities. Thus, your financial problem, your declining grade point average, and your extracurricular activities may be interred – related.

Table 1. Steps In the Scientific Method and their equivalents

In Management Decision Making

The Scientific Method

Management Decision Making

1. Define the problem

2. Collect data

3. Develop hypotheses

4. Test hypotheses

5. analyze results

6. Draw conclusion

1. Define the decision Problem

2.Search for data and information

3. Generate alternative sources of action

4. Analyze feasible alternatives

5. Selects the best source of action

6. Implement the decision and evaluate results

It is important to collect relevant data and sort them out in such a way that they will provide information for decision making. For example, you may want to gather information about the different workplaces, wage rates, working conditions, type of work, potential value of the work experience, and perhaps, from some of your friends who have worked at these places, the personality of the boss you have to work for.

Step 3. Generate Alternative Courses of Action:

The next step to generate alternative courses of action that could be taken for the decision problem. Most people, limit their search for alternatives to those that are obvious and readily available. It is important to generate additional alternatives so that all feasible courses of action can be evaluated. For example, in searching for part-time work, you may want to check the local and state employment offices in addition to the classified ads.

Step 4. Analyze Feasible Alternatives:

Armed with the information about the problem and the available courses of action, you must now get to analyzing alternatives. The primary standards to be used in the analyses are the objective criteria—the things that you would like to accomplish. For example, you may set several criteria about your part-time work such as wage rate, the number of hours you can work per week, work schedule (no graveyard shift, please), coordination with your class schedule and with important extracurricular activities, working conditions, and value of experience.

You should then evaluate each alternative against the objective criteria. You can easily eliminate several alternatives that are clearly inferior to others. Such alternatives are often referred to as 'dominated solutions. In order to evaluate the non-dominated alternatives, you may wish to use priorities for the objective criteria. For example, suppose you have the following simple list of priorities written down on the back of an envelope.

Property 1: Total pay per week

Property 2: No conflict with class schedule

Property 3: Value of experience

Property 4: No midnight shift

Property 5: No conflict with extracurricular activities

Property 6: Working condition

Property 7: Working hours per week

Now you should be able to further eliminate some alternatives on the list.

Step 5. Select the best cause of action:

Once the analysis of alternatives is carpeted, you can make a decision by selecting the best course of action. The final decision will be based on a number of considerations, some qualitative and some judgmental. For example, how Mach money you can make in a week as a quantitative criterion. On the other hand, the value of experience working conditions, considerable working schedule, and conflict with other activities represent judgmental consideration. Evaluation of decision criteria in terms of their priorities to you is perhaps the most sufficient way to select the best course of action.

When we have a set of objective criteria we want to achieve, we often get into a tangle of trade-o's. in other words, sometimes we can achieve an important objective if we give up something else. You know exactly what we mean when you consider your flourishing social activities provides additional information which may be valuable in selecting the best course of action.

Step 6. Implement the decision and evaluate results:

Decision making means taking a certain action. Implementation of action plans is the final phase of decision making. However, we do not stop there. We Synonyms for the term management science are numerous. A suitable substitute is 'operations research' and other terms such as 'systems analysis', decision analysis, and 'decision science' are also used. We have decided to use the term 'management science' in this book because we are basically concerned with the systematic analysis of management decision problems. There is no organizational barrier lor management science application. In other words, we can use management science for decision problems in Government, military service, business and industry, academic institutions, health care organizations, and many other areas.

10.5 HOW MANAGERS ACTUALLY MAKE DECISIONS

Now that we know something about rational decision making and management science, let us focus our attention on how managers actually make decision in real world situations. Management science points the manager to unitize a scientific or analytical approach to problem solving. We believe management science has contributed more toward to acceptance of purpose of purpose-oriented management (often referred to as management to objective) than is usually appreciated by managers and scholars.

The role of management science is especially important today because of the following factors;

The technology being used by organizations is getting more sophisticated every day (chatmate, electronics, lasers, industrial robots, etc.)

There is an increasing shortage of energy and critical materials (fossil fuels, certain vital methods etc.)

Managerial problems are not only complex but are becoming even more important (oil importing decisions that involve international relations, development of computer-based information systems, design of the MX missile system etc.)

The problems managers face is often new and there is no benefit to be drawn decision making. Thus, managers attempt to forecast future problems and plan ahead of the problems that actually energy (public transits systems, synthetic fuel development, research on electrical cars etc.)

Although we recognize the importance of management science in analyzing important problems, also realize that management's is a human process. There exists an enormous gap between the manager's aspirations for using the scientific method for problem solving and actually of trying to sort out a big mess tram a disorganized chain or random events. In reality, the manager is not like an economic person who is totally rational and effective in utilizing the scientific method for decision making.

Recent developments and broad empirical investigations strongly indicate that the concept of for economic person cannot be applied today's managers. There is no evidence that the manager! Capable of performing completely rational analysis of complex decision problems. We also know that the manager's value system is not identical o=to in conformity with the organizations objective. Furthermore, the manager in reality is quite incapable of identifying the optimum choice, if there exists such a thing, either because of the lack of analytical ability o because of the complexity of the problem.

As we discussed earlier, the descriptive theories of decision making are concerned with how decisions are actually made in reality. The descriptive theories are based on an abundance of empirical data that propose the now celebrated concept of "bounded rationally". Herbert A Sinn on states that under bounded rationally, individual decision makers strive to be as efficient as possible in achieving organizational objectives given their limited Information processing abilities. Clearly, bounded rationality does not mean irrationality. The decision maker employs an 'approximate' or 'intentional' rationality in the process of attempting to do the best to achieve organizational goals within the given set of constraints.

Define the Establish Search for Select Reinforce

Problem feasible satisfying the best decision

Objective solution solution maker's Decision

Criteria

Adjust

Objective

Criteria

As we can imagine, management science models developed the unrealistic conditions of complete rationality have very limited real-world implications. In order to Implement decision models, then, either we must sufficiently simplify the model so that the optimum solution can be easily derived, or we must design a realistic model and seek satisfactory solutions. The first is the traditional approach, whereas tot second approach attempts to retain a richer set of properties of the real decision environment by giving up optimization. Although the two approaches are quite different, they are both 'satisficing' approaches based on the concept of bounded rationality and have been idly applied by the management scientists. The satisfying approach attempts to obtain a good solution that is sufficiently satisfactory for a complex decision problem.

The global optimization model based on single objective criterion. (e.g., Cost minimization or profit minimization) is often unrealistic. Perhaps the most practical way to develop a decision model would be to replace the abstract global optimization goal with tangible and measurable sub goals. These sub goals. These sub goals can be formulated on the basis of certain aspiration levels that are related to the organizational goals. Once a decision alternative satisfies a set of aspirations (or at least satisfies important ones.) the search activity could be terminated. The satisfying model based on aspiration level allows for a bounded rational cotton by permitting reasonable amounts of analytical effort and Incomplete information about the decision environment.

In reality, managers make decisions based not sooty on solutions derived from management science models. As a matter of fact, management science models are often used to generate new information or to answer "What it" questions. Based on lur decision so far, we can present the decision-making process sown to figure 2.

10.6 THE ROLE OF MANAGEMENT SCIENCE:

If managers are not completely rational and systematic in decision making, what then Is the role of management science? We can quickly come up with a number of important problems that we have not been able to solve with powerful computer-based management science models; the world population explosion, pollution, the energy shortage, international tension, hunger, decreasing natural resources, and so on. In the role of the Devil's Advocated, let us ask ourselves what the world would be like today without systematic analysis of these complex problems. We are sure that the world would be in a not situation than it is today. We believe management science will play an increasingly more important in the future, precisely because of the manager's limited ability and rationality.

We are now quite comfortable with the nation that decision making must consider environment factors., multiple objectives, satisfying, and bounded rationality. We should not view management science as a panacea for managerial decision problems. Decision making is and always will be based on hurt judgment, intuition, creativity and perhaps courage, in addition to many systematic approaches. Muscle the disillusionment and criticisms of management science is the result of unrealistic expectations on part of those who use it.

Management Science plays the following important roles:

Purpose-oriented Decision Making:

Management science applications requires an organization to purpose oriented. Work activities are planned and carried out according to organizational objectives ran than simply rationalizing habits by saying. "We have always done it this way". "What does this act contribute towards important organizational objectives" is frequently asked the before resources committed.

The basic approach of management should be to purpose long-range achievement of organizational purpose, not to seek only short-term monetary objectives. Rhagades and Jabiru Management Professor at Harvard University, contend that one of the primary reasons for the final and productivity woes of many American Corporations is their emphasis on short-term profit object often at the expenses of long-term organizational goals. Management science can be salary coordinating management functions for purpose-oriented decision making in a long-term perspective.

Information and Analysis-based Decision Making:

Decision making based on management seen requires an efficient information processing system. With the ever-increasing complexity of environment and its vital impact on the organization's survival information management beet extremely important. Accurate and timely information must be processed in order to predict the state of affairs with an acceptable degree of accuracy.

Management science models can be used to generate additional information. The use of comp for everyday decision making is becoming more prevalent. With the availability of inexpensive but powerful micro and mini computers, even small organizations can effectively use management science.

Decision Making for Multiple Objectives:

Managers should be vitally concerned with the anal multiple objectives, not only with their formulation but with their priorities and trade-offs. We are too aware of the ever-increasing pressure for the simultaneous satisfaction of such factors as Govern regulations, economic optimization, industrial relations, and customers' demands. Managers must the direct conflict between the organization's economic survival and the other objectives that are not social responsibilities.

Managers are being held increasingly more accountable for the legitimacy of their priorities, and resolutions of the conflicts among the objectives of the various interest groups. Thus, we expect to see more widespread application of systematic approaches in dealing with multiple goal their trade-offs. Computer based interactive an approaches using management science models are wider applications in objective formulation and decision making.

Increased Emphasis on Productivity:

The essential purpose of management science is to be the efficiency of the organization. In order to improve the effectiveness to the management process important areas should be evaluated:

1. Productivity of human resources.

2. Effective management of capital and materials, and

3. Efficient decision-making process.

Management science, can make important contributions to all three areas. We believe that the effective utilization of human resources is the key to the survival and prosperity of the organization.

Increased Attention to Group Behavior:

As we focus attention on the effective utilization of human resources, group decision making behavior will become increasingly more important. Most management science projects are interred disciplinary in nature. In other words, people from several different department such as production, finance, marketing, and personal would work together to solve a common problem. It has been pointed out by many scholars that one of the important reasons for the poor showing of American workers in the world productivity race is management's failure to recognize the importance of worker's group behavior. Harvard sociologist Ezra R Vogel, in his book Japan as number one: Lessons for America, contends that the phenomenal productivity increase of Japanese workers is due to their group-conscious., behavior patterns that seek to belong to groups, and group loyalty and confidence in group objectives are driving forces. Group conscious behavior, especially the importance of the sense of shared purpose for organizational effectiveness, should receive greater attention from management in the United States.

Efficient Management of Capital, Energy and Material:

With the increasing scarcity and cost of acquiring capital, energy and material, the effective management of these resources is almost as important as the management of human resources. As economist Martin Feldstein point out, the American economy suffer from a lack of capital formation due to the low savings rate of the American people. He singles out inflation and government taxes that penalize savings are the main causes of declining savings. Efficient management of capital energy, and materials requires systematic approaches based on computer bass' formation systems and management science. Cost savings from these resources represent a 100 per cent contribution to profits while cost savings in other areas (e.g., marketing channels) may represent only very small net contribution to profits.

More Systematic Contingency Management:

In the future we will probably see more drastic changes in the environment than we have in the past. We will face a shortage of energy, materials, water, clear air, and many other resources. We will also see some important technology break troughs: cheaper and more powerful microcomputers, new method for harnessing energy, new transportation methods. We can jilts expect many political and economic exercises in the international area. All these changes will have varying degree of impact on the organizations.

However, an organization cannot be totally relative to situations, functioning without plans. Nor can it be totally productive, with every possible contingency planned, for changing situations. But with the aid of management targets and the means to get there, with the availability of information systems, management science models and computational facilities, contingency management can be more systematic and orderly.

Close International with External Factors:

The management process is an open system. Its breathers in external factors in the form of environmental constraints, needs, and information. The use of management science requires such information that the entire system remains current ad effective. Thus, management science necessitates that the organization have closer interactions with external forces: government agencies, informational situations, socio-economic factors of the environment, consumer concerns, changing market situations and the like.

10.7 SUMMARY

This chapter has provided a board introduction to management science in terms of its meaning, role, history. You are not expected to be an expert in management sciences after reading this chapter but you should have a good feel for what management science is about. You should also have learned to use several new jargonistic terms such as optimization, the concept of economic person, scientific method, satisfying and management information systems.

10.8 REFERENCES

Introduction to Management Science, Sang M Lee the Dryden Press (Pages 2-15) Topic in Management Science Robert E. Market Land. John Witty & Sons Inc.

10.9 QUESTIONS FOR SELF ASSESSMENT

1. What is the difference between management and management science?

2. Is management an art or science? Discuss your own ideas.

10.10 QUESTIONS

1. What are the advantages and disadvantages of the scientific methods?

2. What is relationship between management science and the systems approach?

3. Discuss the three important roles of management science?

Bibliography

1. T. R. Banga, N. K. Agarwal, S. C. Sharma, Industrial Engineering and Management Publish eScience, Khanna Publishers, Delhi o1989. 1 to 7
2. Richard McVaugh's, Introduction to industrial engineering. The lowa state university press, USA, Second edition. Pages 5-9, 33 and 34.
3. W. Grant Ireson and Engine L. Grant, Hand book of Industrial Engineering and Management, Prentice Hall of India Private limited, New Delhi, 1917 pages 1121-1183.
4. International labour office, Geneva, Introduction of work study, universal Book corporation, Bombay, third (revised) Edition. Pages 3 to 16
5. K.C. Jain and L.N. Aggarwal, production planning control and Industrial management, Khanna Publishers, Delhi First Edition. 595 to 609.
6. David Sumanth, Productivity engineering and Management, MC Glow-Hill Book company pages 3 to 7, 76 to 228, 303 – 329.
7. International Labour Office, Geneva, Introduction to Work Study, Universal Book Corporation, Bombay. Third (revised) Edition, Pages 29 to 183.
8. Ralph M. Blanes, Motion and Time Study Design and Measurement of work, John Wiley and sons, Inc. U.S.A. Sixth edition, pages 3 to 31, 63 to 161, 169 to 189.
9. Cycasin and L.N.Aggarwal, Production planning control and industrial Management, Khanna Publishers, Delhi, Pages 610 to 718.
10. W. Grant Ireson and Engane L. Grant, Hand Book of Industrial Engineering and Management, Prentice-Hall of India Private Limited, New Delhi, 1971, pages 283 to 353.
11. International Labour Office, Geneva, Introduction to Work Study, Third (Revised)
12. Edition, Universal Book Corporation, Bombay, pages 187 to 271.
13. K.C. Jain and L.N. Aggarwal, production Planning Control and Industrial Management, Khanna Publishers, Delhi, First Edition, pages 718 to 729
14. Ralph Barnes, Motion a Time Study Design and Measurement of Work, John Wiley and Sons, U.S.A., Sixth Edition, Pages 342-417.
15. Elwood's S. Buffer, Modern Production/Operations Management, John Wiley and Sons, U.S.A.., Sixth Edition, pages 621 to 637.
16. International Labour Office, Geneva, introduction of Work Study, Universal Book Corporation, Bombay, Third (Revised) Edition, pages 29-45, 79-373.
17. Ralph Barnes, Motion and Time Study Design and Measurement of Work, John Wiley and Sons Inc., U.S.A., Sixth Edition, Pages 32-99, 342-417.
18. Ralph Currier Davis, Industrial Organisation and Management, Halper & Brothers, New York, Third Edition, Pages 397-433.
19. T.R. Banga, N.K. Agarwal, S.C. Sharma, Industrial Engineering and Management Science, Khanna Publishers, Delhi, 1989, Pages 8-53.
20. "Motion and Time Study-Design and measurement of work Ralph Barnes, 6th edition, John Wiley and Sons, INC (pages 221-306).
21. "Introduction to Works Study", International labour office, Universal book corporation, (pages 154-170)
22. "Motion and Time Study – Design and measurement of work" Ralf. M. Barnes, sixth edition, John-Wiley & sons, Inc. (pages209-211).
23. "Quality control – a practical approach" Dale H. Esterified, Prentice Hall; INC., (Pages 1-94).
24. "Quality control-a practical approach" Dale. B e starfield. Pritchel, Inc. (pages 117-234).
25. "Operations Management" Kostas N Devastates, Mc-Graw-Hill, International Book co.,

26. Introduction to Management Science, Sang M Lee the Dryden Press (Pages 2-15) Topic in Management Science Robert E. Market Land. John Witty & Sons Inc.

27. Sang M. Lee Introduction of Management Science. Lee S. M. Moore L. J. Introduction to Decision Science New York 1975.